From the Mists of Eden

From the Mists of Eden

Stories from My Family from Long Ago

JAMES AYERS

WIPF & STOCK · Eugene, Oregon

FROM THE MISTS OF EDEN
Stories from My Family from Long Ago

Copyright © 2012 James Ayers. All rights reserved. Except for brief quotations in critical publications or reviews, no part of this book may be reproduced in any manner without prior written permission from the publisher. Write: Permissions, Wipf and Stock Publishers, 199 W. 8th Ave., Suite 3, Eugene, OR 97401.

Wipf & Stock
An Imprint of Wipf and Stock Publishers
199 W. 8th Ave., Suite 3
Eugene, OR 97401
www.wipfandstock.com

ISBN 13: 978-1-61097-330-4

Manufactured in the U.S.A.

All scripture quotations, unless otherwise indicated, are taken from the Holy Bible, New International Version®, NIV®. Copyright ©1973, 1978, 1984 by Biblica, Inc.™ Used by permission of Zondervan. All rights reserved worldwide.

to my daughter Rachel,
who has taught me much about storytelling.

Contents

1. Then God Remembered 1
2. Tell Me Your Dreams 11
3. At Your Heels 31
4. Moriah 49
5. Get Out! 63
6. From the Mists of Eden 85
7. The Story of the Do-Over Box 97
8. Sometimes It Causes Me to Tremble 111
9. Days When the Lord Didn't Tell the Truth 121
10. Prophet for Hire 137
11. River Jordan 151

1

Then God Remembered

ONCE UPON A TIME there was an old man. He sat in silence in his chair, there in the corner of the parlor at the rest home. If you looked closely, you could tell that in his time he must have been strong and good-looking. Not any more. It was sad, a little embarrassing, really, but he looked pretty seedy as he sat there. Why does life have to decay that way? Ah well: complain if you want, but life is what it is.

One day my Aunt Shefra went to visit this old man. I guess I should tell you that in my family everyone is an Aunt or an Uncle—that's just the way we are. Well, anyone who is the same age as you is a cousin; and those who are a dozen or more years younger than you are nieces and nephews, which makes you an aunt or uncle to them. You might know the details—Uncle Mike is my mother's brother's wife's grandfather's baby sister's second son. Or you might not be the kind of person who keeps track of all those details: you just know it's Uncle Mike.

So Aunt Shefra isn't literally my Aunt, even though that's what everyone my age and younger actually calls her. And her name isn't literally Shefra, either, even though that's what everyone still alive actually calls her. Her mother named her Shellie Frances, and her parents and older relatives called her that—never Shellie, always Shellie Frances—but when she was a young girl her friends took the first syllable off her first and middle names and glued them together to form Shefra, and that's what everyone has called her for years now. I like it. It's not like anybody else's name.

Aunt Shefra felt a little nervous, when she went to visit that old man in the rest home. She had just been elected a Deacon, and the Deacons had agreed at their last meeting that one of the duties of Deacons was to visit and care for the lonely, sick, and shut-in. Aunt Shefra believed that: she had determined that she was going to go to the rest home and make this visit this afternoon, and so she had walked up to him as he sat on his chair in the corner of the parlor of the rest home, and she had offered up her cheeriest greeting. The old man made no response at all. That made her a little more nervous, but she had already decided she was going to give this her very best. She introduced herself, and tried to strike up some kind of conversation by asking him how he was feeling. It didn't work. She thought maybe he couldn't hear, so she said it all over again, louder. Still no response. So she leaned forward, nearly shouting her greeting into his ear. But he did not speak, did not look at her, did not move.

I suppose lots of people would have just shrugged at this point and headed for home. Or maybe they would just sit in silence for a few minutes or read a quick Bible verse, and then say, "Well, I just wanted to say Hi, I'll see you again some time soon." But for some reason Aunt Shefra decided not to let the awkwardness of the moment chase her away. She wasn't quite sure why she decided that. Somehow it just didn't feel right to give up this soon. She said some more about herself, told a little about her family and her job. It made no difference. She commented on the weather. Still nothing. Then she tried, "Tell me about yourself."

Maybe because of her perseverance, or maybe because of the question, he seemed to rouse a bit. It was such a little response, she wasn't sure if that glimmer of a reaction was really there or just in her imagination; but she wanted to hope that maybe he was trying to reply, or at least communicate something. So she said it again: "Tell me about yourself." His mouth moved; Aunt Shefra was sure that he was trying to say something. She bent close; she focused all her attention, as he worked to speak. Finally the words came out, words that trembled with struggle and ache: "I don't remember."

One quavering sentence is not a lot to pin your hopes on, but as a new Deacon, Aunt Shefra was determined, and she came back next week and tried again. She kept on, week by week. Sometimes she was in a hurry and just breezed in, said hello, pressed his hand for a moment, and went her way. Sometimes she would stay for a while and converse, even though it made no difference at all that she could see, for on many days the old man made no response at all. But other times Aunt Shefra thought she might be on to something, because she'd get some kind of reaction. Most often without any words: just a look, a mumble, or a nod.

And then, every once in a while, it would happen. It might be after she had asked a question like, "Tell me about your family" or "Can you tell me what you used to do for a living?" She would see him working to articulate what he wanted to say. Could it be, please God, that this time he would manage to answer? And indeed he did answer: but it was once again those three plaintive words, in that tremulous voice: "I don't remember."

How long would you think this could go on?

With Aunt Shefra, resolute in her deaconship, it continued for six months. Then those six months grew into a year. Then two years. Week by week Aunt Shefra faithfully went to see this old man. Because she was interested, she did some research. She found out about his family. She found out about his career. Then when she went see him, she would say, "I was reading about what you used to do a few years back." Or "I found out some interesting facts about your family." And then she would ask, "Can you tell me the story of how that all came about?" And then the light in his eyes, and the struggle to put it into words: and then, again, the "I don't remember."

I sometimes wonder how long I would keep on trying, in a situation like this. Would I go on for two years, hoping for the miracle? I suspect I would come to the point of saying, "It's no use. I've tried and tried. I still really do believe there's something there. But most of the time I don't get anything at all by way of response; and even at the best of times I can't be sure I'm even getting through. Maybe 'I don't remember' is all he remembers how to say. And even if it isn't, even if he's still there, I just don't know if I've got the endurance to keep coming back, week after week, knowing that there's a pretty good chance that it isn't making any difference at all."

And really, why wouldn't a person come to the point of saying that? Suppose you managed to keep on faithfully checking in, week by week, for three years, or five, or more: that's a pretty heroic commitment, and evidence of a deeply compassionate heart. But even with that, it would certainly be understandable that you would end up saying, "There are limits to this, you know. I've done all I know how to do. I just can't continue any longer."

Somehow, my Aunt Shefra never quite said that. As she kept going by to visit with the old man, somewhere along the line it became clear to her that even though this wasn't happening quickly—and even though it maybe wasn't ever going to happen at all—she was nevertheless in it for the long haul. She asked herself why, and she could not really come up with an answer: she could only acknowledge that she was going to continue, and that was that, whether or not she could ever explain why.

Once she had reached that conclusion, the next step was obvious. She began to bring her children with her. Ha ha, I remember how much they complained about that! They couldn't believe their mother would make them do this, go visit this old man they didn't know anything about. Why should they have to take part in this? She was the deacon, not them, and it was boring, it was creepy, it was So Unfair! But with the same persistence with which she had kept coming to visit the old man, she persisted with them as well. She taught them the stories she had learned from her research about the old man. She taught them how to ask the questions about his life, how to talk to him even if he said nothing in reply. She taught them to be faithful in coming to visit, week by week. She taught them all this: so that when she had died and gone to heaven, they would be there, teaching their children, who would teach their children, who would teach their children, on to the third and fourth generation, to keep persevering in faithfulness, coming to visit with this old man, in the expectation that some day, some day, no matter how distant, the day would come when he would say, "I remember!"

I sometimes wonder whether the kingdom of God is like that. What do you think? Perhaps the kingdom of God is like an old man in a nursing home, with a deacon and her family that come to visit him; he is beloved from generation to generation, and yet he does not remember. From generation to generation God's people remain faithful in obedience, in prayer, in hope that the day will come when God will stand forth, remember his people in their need, and work great miracles to save them and sustain them: but in the meantime, we just keep waiting, faithfully, for God to remember. Is that what God is like?

It is, at any rate, what my family is like. It is part of our consciousness that we live as a family that is many generations deep. My great-great-grandparents are my family; and their great-great-grandparents are as well. Their story is my story. My great-great-grandchildren have not been born; but my story is their story, and their story is mine. I have heard that there are families where people don't think of themselves this way; I do know that our family has not always gotten it right. But down the generations we have come to know that this is how we are to think of ourselves, and so we do: and because we do, we understand ourselves this way, more and more strongly. The stories of who we are and what we have done and how we did it and how it happened to us: we understand that these are our stories. Whether it happened many generations ago or just last week, we own the stories. They are our stories. And in a special sense, the stories own us, too. Often the stories that happened last week only really make sense when we think about them in light of other stories, stories from centuries ago. And so we remember the stories, and we tell the stories to each other, from generation to generation.

So when Aunt Shefra was a teenager, she became interested in a story from long ago about another aunt. This aunt had almost the same name, and that's what caught Aunt Shefra's attention, and motivated her to learn the story from many generations ago about Aunt Shiphrah.

Once upon a time there was a young couple, Zvi and Ilana. Ilana was expecting their first child, and she was scared. She knew how babies are born. She knew it was the most natural thing in the world. She knew that she had come into the world this way, and so had all her brothers and sisters, and so had all the children laughing and playing outside her window in the evening, just before their mothers called them inside for supper. But she also knew that many women died in childbirth. Including her own mother, who had died when Ilana's baby sister was born.

And so when her labor started, Ilana tried to remain calm and let the contractions do their work, without becoming too anxious. But she did not succeed: she was scared. The labor pains were only uncomfortable when they began; they didn't really hurt, not badly, not yet. But Ilana felt the fear starting to build up inside her, the terrible dread that these pains were going to tear her apart. And so she told Zvi to send for Aunt Shiphrah, who was a midwife.

The contractions had increased in intensity, and the interval between them had shortened, during the time it took for the neighbor boy to run to fetch Aunt Shiphrah. Even so, soon enough she came bustling in through the doorway, full of competence and assurance. Over the years Aunt Shiphrah had perfected a blend of bossiness and compassion: when Aunt Shiphrah told you to do something, you did it; but you did it in the knowledge that she really cared about you. So when Aunt Shiphrah said to Ilana, "Listen to me, girl. I want you to breathe along with me," Ilana started matching Aunt Shiphrah's slow rhythmic breathing: and her panic started to ebb away.

Aunt Shiphrah turned to Zvi. "Outside, nephew," she commanded. "Men are good for a lot of things, but this isn't one of them. Out you go. Send me in a couple of aunts to help out, that's a good boy." And Zvi was out the door, just like that: feeling awkward to be kicked out of his own house, feeling scared and wanting to be there holding hands with his bride and helping somehow, and feeling relieved that in this moment when everything was outside his control, someone with the experience and wisdom of Aunt Shiphrah was in charge: all those mixed feelings rolled into one bundle of confusion.

It took a few more hours, but indeed the baby was born, a healthy son. Both mother and baby were fine. The men were all shouting and laughing out in the street as if they were the ones who had done something strong and noble, and they were pounding Zvi on the back and congratulating him. The other aunts were fussing around the house, making sure Ilana was comfortable, and cooing over the baby, whom Zvi and Ilana named Ethan, which means *enduring*.

And on her way home, Aunt Shiphrah got arrested.

The Pharoah had made a law. These were the days when our family lived in the land of Egypt, and even though we were all well respected at first, that respect had eroded as the generations had passed. Somehow all our freedom had evaporated and we had been turned into slaves. The Pharoah had made a law that said that Aunt Shiphrah was supposed to let newborn babies live, if they were girls, but if the newborn was a boy, she was supposed to—make it look like the baby was stillborn. Really it meant that she had to kill him; but it was supposed to look like one of those great sad moments when a baby is born dead. There had been a special meeting about this: Aunt Shiphrah and Aunt Puah and all the rest of the midwives had had to attend, and the officials had explained this new law to them.

Aunt Shiphrah had spoken up. "We are all loyal workers here," she said. "We understand what it is that you are telling us to do. And we understand that in political situations like this, it sometimes forces people to do things they would rather not do. We understand that. And so, speaking for my sisters and me, we want you to know that we will certainly render to the Pharoah's command all the obedience that it deserves."

And all the other midwives nodded, with such a sense of humility and dedication that the officials thought that the midwives had said they would obey this new law.

But then the midwives went back to midwifing, delivering healthy boys and girls alike. And among themselves, in the privacy of their own gatherings, they mocked the notion that the Pharoah and his officials could make them kill their own nephews.

For of course the midwives had recognized that the officials had not said everything. They had not stated the purpose of this new law. But the purpose was obvious enough to Aunt Shiphrah and the other midwives. In just a few years, all those baby girls would grow up, but there wouldn't be any boys left in the family; and so all the girls would end up married to Egyptian boys. And our family would no longer be *our* family: we would be scattered among thousands of Egyptian families.

The intention of the new law was the assimilation of our family. And that meant the destruction of our family. Our family would cease to exist. It would be the loss of our identity. The loss of our stories. The loss of our God.

Our identity as a family is tied up in the stories we tell about our family: and especially our identity comes out in the stories we tell about how our family has learned from God, and loved God, and been loved by God. Sometimes we have managed to follow God's call quite well. Sometimes we have done quite badly. But always, always, there are stories: stories about how God spoke, stories about how God led us, in the midst of the times when we were doing well and in the midst of the times when we were doing badly. Always there are stories about what God showed us about ourselves, about life, about one another.

Well, almost always.

There are no stories about God, from this time in the life of our people. It is a puzzle to me. We were ordinary people in those days, as far as I can tell, about the same as what we have been all down the generations. Here in our day we have a few saints and a few scoundrels, and the rest of us somewhere in the middle, and I am sure it has been the same in every generation.

In every generation we have taught our children and grandchildren the stories of God. We taught them to pray. We prayed with them and for them. In those days, in the days of Aunt Shiphrah and Aunt Puah, we cried to the Lord, we called on our God for deliverance from the cruel oppression of those who held us in bondage. But no deliverance came. God did not answer. As far as anyone could tell, God had forgotten us.

We could not quite say it that way. We knew that God would never forget us. We have known that, in every generation. "God is an ever-present help in trouble"—we believed that. "I am with you always"—we believed that.

But there have been times when that was not the way we experienced it.

In faith, in confidence, our family has believed with all our hearts that God will never ever forget us. But in the depths of hard times, that hasn't always been the way it feels. There have been times when people in our family have cried out, "O God! Why have you forgotten me?" And they have poured out their souls in deep lament: "How long, O Lord? Will you forget me forever?"

Our family lived in the land of Egypt for four hundred thirty years. We know the stories about how we got there; and we know the stories about how we left there. But although we lived there for four centuries, we have only the briefest of stories about that time. We only know a few names of the members of our family from that time, brave women like Aunt Shiphrah and Aunt Puah.

When the officials arrested Aunt Shiphrah, they were pretty upset, and it was clear why: they had discovered that she wasn't following the new law. They knew she had been at the meeting where the midwives had been given their new instructions. They even remembered that she had spoken up there. So she knew the new law: when a baby was born, if it was a girl she was supposed to let her live; but if it was a boy, she was supposed to 'discover' that the baby was stillborn. But she wasn't doing that part. Why not? Why was she letting those baby boys live? That's what they wanted to know.

So Aunt Shiphrah looked at the officials, and said, "I've never had the chance to do it. The women in our family, they go into labor, and out pops the baby, just like that. Sometimes they never even have time to send for me; and sometimes they send for me but the baby is already born and the mother is back up on her feet and everyone has seen that the baby is alive and well, long before I ever get in the door."

That was a lie.

She told it well, though. Even though she had been on her way home from delivering a baby boy when she got arrested, Aunt Shiphrah looked those officials right in the eye and told them this lie.

To disguise it, she went right on talking. "Now, your Egyptian girls are more delicate. I sometimes have to work with them for quite a few hours before the baby finally puts in an appearance. Why, just last week one of your Egyptian girls was in labor, and they called me in. She was just a tiny little thing, and I could tell it was a big baby. Took a day and a half. Poor little girl, she was about worn out by the time the baby finally arrived. Well, of course, she's from a well-to-do family, she hasn't had to work hard day by day. Like I said, delicate. Not like our girls. Well, I could tell that this particular delivery was going to take a long time. So what I did was . . ."

The officials interrupted her at about this point, because they didn't really want to hear all the details about the delivery of this baby. And so they sent Aunt Shiphrah on home.

So Aunt Shiphrah and Aunt Puah and the other midwives continued to help in the births of girls and boys; and then in time they grew old, and died. As did all the others of their generation. Our men worked in the fields, worked on building projects for the Pharoahs, worked at whatever tasks the slave-masters commanded them; and they grew old and died. Our women worked in the fields as well, and worked in their homes and in the homes of the Egyptians, worked at whatever tasks they were commanded; and they grew old and died. And we were faithful, all those years. With devotion, with desperation, in every generation we called on God to help us, to set us free from this slavery. But God did not answer. Our children grew up, had babies who grew up and had babies of their own; and then they died, too. Decade followed decade, century followed century, and we kept on calling on God to set us free. But God did not answer.

And so we lived in poverty, in hardship, in slavery, from generation to generation. We suffered and groaned under this bondage, and our cry went up to God. And then the story says this most remarkable thing: then God remembered. God remembered the covenant he had made with our family; he saw the pain we were enduring as slaves, and he was concerned.

After four hundred years, God remembered us.

Listen to me, my children. This is one of the stories of our family. It is a story that we don't tell as often as we should. It is a story that tells us who we are: we are the family that endured, when life was bitter and hard. It is a story that tells us we are the family that would not give up on who we are, when suffering and slavery was our lot, from generation to generation. It is a story that tells us we are the family that remained faithful when it seemed that even our God had forgotten us. It is a story that tells us we are a family that kept on praying, kept on believing, kept on crying out to God for deliverance, kept on teaching our children how to call on God, even when there was no evidence that any of it was making any difference at all.

And it is a story that tells us that our God did indeed remember us.

Hear this story, my nieces and nephews. Somewhere in the depths of your heart you believe, as do I, that God is with us always, and that in every circumstance the presence of our Lord will comfort and sustain us. This is part of our story, now and always, and even though you have your doubts and your worries, in some inner place in your soul you know that it is true.

Yet you are well aware that our people have not always experienced it this way. There have been times in the heritage of our family, and there will be such times again, when the most honest assessment anyone could make would be a heart cry of anguish: "O God, why have you forgotten me?" There have been times in the heritage of our family, and there will be such times again, when the lament in our souls could only be, "How long, O Lord! Will you forget us forever?"

And in those times, this is the story that you will want to tell. It is the story of Aunt Shiphrah, who spoke across all the intervening years to the heart of Aunt Shefra, who then told it to others and to me: the story of how our family endured for more than four hundred years when it seemed that God had forgotten us.

And then God remembered. God remembered us, and sent us a deliverer. I will tell you the story of that deliverer in a little while. But first I need to tell you how it came about that our family ended up in such bondage for four centuries.

2

Tell Me Your Dreams

It had not been a good year for Uncle Joe.

The boss's wife's name was Zelicha, and she had The Look. She had the clothes; she had the face; she had the figure; she had the walk: and she knew how to use all of them. She could gaze at you with such innocence in her eyes, as if she had just no idea that there was anything about her that would turn men's heads. And she could gaze at you with the mocking half-smile that said she knew exactly what men were thinking they'd like to do with her. Zelicha knew she was one hot number, and she liked it. She had The Look. And Uncle Joe was just like every other 18-year-old boy in the world whose blood has caught fire whenever he sees a woman with The Look.

But there was no chance at all, for Uncle Joe. The woman was probably ten years older than he was. *And* she would already have been way beyond Uncle Joe's league even if she was just seventeen. *And* she was already married. *And* she was married to the boss. *And* the boss was a colonel in the army; *and* the boss was a jealous older man with a trophy wife. So it didn't really matter how strongly he felt the flame in his soul when Zelicha walked by; there was just no way in the world that anything was ever going to happen.

And then it did.

It started with Zelicha making little remarks. "My, Joey, you certainly are an attractive young buck, aren't you? Just look at those muscles!" She'd say something like that, and Uncle Joe would blush; and then she would wink at him and say, "I can't help thinking how lucky some girl is going to be, when she gets held in those big strong arms, and gets to kiss that pretty mouth." And then as she walked away down the hall she'd glance back over her shoulder and wiggle just a little bit. And then she'd grin with that I-know-what-you're-thinking grin and say, "Maybe it's going to happen pretty soon."

Uncle Joe didn't have a lot of experience with this sort of thing. Truth to tell, he didn't have any at all. He didn't want to admit that; and so at first he had tried to look worldly-wise and to laugh along with Zelicha's comments. Then he decided that he was embarrassed, the whole situation was terribly awkward, and he wasn't gaining anything by pretending otherwise. This was the boss's wife, and Uncle Joe just knew he would be in a lot of trouble if the boss ever walked in on one of these flirty conversations.

And so he did his best to steer clear of Zelicha, keep his nose clean and do his job. He liked his job, and he was good at it: and so he worked to stay focused on it. The boss had started him as an errand boy, but the office manager had quickly noticed Uncle Joe's aptitude with numbers and after just seven weeks had put him to work as a junior accountant. About six months after that, the office manager had left to take a new position, and the boss had made Uncle Joe acting office manager. And so there he was, not yet nineteen years old and day by day he was actually running the whole business. He figured with some luck he could get himself a girlfriend, get married, raise a family; maybe this could turn out to be a pretty good life.

But Zelicha wasn't through with him. It seemed like every time she got the chance, she would speak to him, always with some suggestive invitation lurking in her words. She would walk in his direction, apparently thinking about something else, completely unaware of how the strap of her dress hovered at the edge of slipping off her shoulder, and not even noticing him until she would glance at him at precisely the right moment so that she could catch him looking. Then she would reach up her hand to adjust the strap, but she would inadvertently miss and the strap would slip just that little bit more; and she would giggle and say something risqué: and then laugh when he blushed. So Uncle Joe learned to turn casually in another direction, to pick up a document and study it, or in some other way to be busy and not notice her: and so she would walk past him and just manage to brush against him so that her sleeve would caress his arm as she went by.

Then one afternoon it happened. The colonel was gone for the day, and no one was around except for Zelicha and Uncle Joe. She came into his office wearing some kind of filmy robe, and looked him full in the face and gave him The Look. She walked straight toward him, rotating her shoulders so that the robe fell to the floor, and Uncle Joe gasped. "You and me, Joey," she said. "We're going to bed. Enough of this coy flirtation. I want some serious action out of you, Joey, and I want it now." She had his shirt bunched up in her left fist, and her right hand started unfastening his shirt buttons.

From the depth of his soul Uncle Joe knew that this was a disaster. "Look, no," he said. "I can't do this. It wouldn't be right. The colonel trusts me; I can't betray his trust this way."

Zelicha had her hand inside his shirt by now, running her palm across his chest, pulling him close, and Uncle Joe did the only thing he could think of. He ran. He ran out of the building. And Zelicha was left standing there, holding his shirt.

Zelicha was not one to shrug off this rejection by recognizing that there were plenty of other pretty boys out there that she could console herself with. When the colonel got home that night, he found Zelicha fully dressed, but the sleeve on her blouse was torn and he could see a bad bruise on her arm. She sobbed out her story about how that acting office manager, what's his name, had tried to rape her; and she had been so scared but she had screamed and he had run off, leaving his shirt behind, and here was the shirt right here to prove the story.

They threw Uncle Joe in prison that night. He wasn't sure what he would say, at the trial; he didn't think anyone would believe him when he told the truth. But he never got a chance to find out, because month after month went by, and there never was a trial.

So it had not been a good year, for Uncle Joe. Indeed, it had already been a bad year, before any of this happened. The bad part had started when his brothers had sold him into slavery.

When he was growing up, Uncle Joe had been the youngest of eleven brothers. The other ten boys all thought he was spoiled rotten, and maybe it was true. His father, Uncle Jacob, certainly seemed to act like he loved this youngest child the best: maybe because Uncle Joe was the last, or maybe because he was the only son of the one woman whom his father really loved.

You see, Uncle Jacob had two wives. Well, actually he kind of had four, but that's a major story all by itself; I won't get into that just now. The important point is that one of these women, Aunt Rachel, was the woman that always owned Uncle Jacob's heart. And she had no children, for just the longest time. When she finally gave birth to a baby, Uncle Jacob doted over this little one, gave him special gifts and special attention, and a fine and fancy coat. Everyone knew that Uncle Jacob loved this one child the best. If you have ever seen sibling rivalry in action, you can predict exactly what effect that had on Uncle Joe's ten brothers.

Then, when Uncle Joe was about fifteen, Aunt Rachel got pregnant again. It was a hard pregnancy, and a hard birth; and Aunt Rachel died just after the baby was born. They named this baby Benny. You might think that this new child would now become the spoiled baby of the family; but Uncle Joe still seemed to have that role. He was still his father's favorite, and it looked like he always would be.

Certainly he dreamed that he always would be. Uncle Joe dreamed that the day would come when he would be like a great king or something, and all his family would recognize just how wonderful and powerful he was. Some dreams are better kept to yourself, when you have ten older brothers who already think you are more trouble than you're worth; but this dream seemed so real, almost like a vision from God instead of just a random dream or a daydream. So Uncle Joe went ahead and told his brothers about this special dream. They were not impressed. They told him he was not only a spoiled brat, he was a spoiled brat with delusions of grandeur.

Then one day, a couple of years later when Uncle Joe was seventeen, Uncle Jacob sent him on an errand to check on the other ten sons, now mostly in their twenties, as they herded the sheep from pasture to pasture across the wilderness. They had moved around quite a bit, moving the flock from one spot to another in search of the best grazing; it took a few days for Uncle Joe to catch up with them. And when he did, they saw their chance. They snatched off his fine and fancy coat; they tied him up; they threw him in an empty pit; and then they sold him to a caravan of slave traders on their way to Egypt.

Being beaten up and thrown into a pit by your brothers, and then sold as a slave: it's hard to think that would be a good way to spend the afternoon. Being transported as a slave in a caravan of slave traders would make a person feel pretty anxious about future prospects. Then when the caravan arrived in Egypt, the slave traders had sold him to an Egyptian army officer.

That could have been just as bad as the rest of it; but the officer had given Uncle Joe a chance, and Uncle Joe had worked his way up from errand boy to junior accountant to acting office manager, and he had thought maybe it was going to be all right. And then that disaster with Zelicha. And now here he was, stuck in prison, maybe forever, for a crime he had not committed.

As I say, it had not been a good year for Uncle Joe.

Being stuck in a dungeon is dull. Nothing good ever happens. Every once in a while someone gets executed. Other than that, life is just dull: dull for the prisoners, dull for the guards, dull for the warden. This can breed resentment among the prisoners and complacency among the guards. The possibility of execution means that there is a constant low-grade fear in the souls of all the prisoners. The possibility of a riot among the prisoners means that there is a constant low-grade fear in the souls of all the guards. Boredom and anxiety, well mixed: probably nothing would happen on any given day, probably today would be just as dull as every other day; and yet it could happen that today would be a day of sudden violence and death.

From day to day and month to month, Uncle Joe lived in a corner of the dungeon. Slowly he got to know the other prisoners; the stories of their lives, how they had ended up in prison, their fears for their families. He had picked up a decent working knowledge of the Egyptian language during his months in the colonel's service; but here in the prison—mostly to keep himself from going insane with boredom—he had made it a point to learn new words and phrases every day. Sometimes he wondered why he bothered. What did it matter, if he could talk fluently to the other prisoners? After all, there were no words or phrases he could ever learn that could be encouraging, in a setting like that. There could be no genuine hope that 'things might get better' or 'things will turn out all right.'

Yet somehow it made a difference for the prisoners that someone would listen to them. As the months passed they began to look to Uncle Joe as a leader. From time to time he actually ended up sorting out some of the petty squabbles between the men. He did this well, and that in turn strengthened the respect and leadership the men accorded to him. So the years went by; and even the warden came to view Uncle Joe as someone he could rely on. A dungeon will always be a dungeon, and boredom and anxiety will always be the lot of prisoners and guards; but whenever there is a little more peace and a little less violence—and therefore a little less anxiety, even if that means a little more boredom—that is probably a good thing. And with Uncle Joe's leadership, that's what they had.

Ten years passed. Uncle Joe had turned 28. For most young men, the decade from 18 to 28 are years of vigor, years of begetting and raising children; these are the years when a young man establishes what he will do with his life: what he will do with the strengths and gifts God has entrusted to him. But Uncle Joe had spent those ten years living in his corner of the dungeon, being a leader of prisoners, helping their small enclosed world become a little more boring and a little less anxious. And then, finally, after all those ten years, something interesting happened.

Two court officers, the chief cupbearer and the chief baker, had gotten themselves in trouble with the king: and with no further ado, they were thrown into the dungeon. Being in prison is an anxious time for anyone, but especially so for court officers; they can hardly expect gentle treatment from the other prisoners. So the warden put them in Uncle Joe's care.

Their worries affected their dreams. Uncle Joe could see their anxiety revealed on their faces, and he asked them about it. "We have had dreams," they told him. "Troubling dreams. We do not know what these dreams might mean."

"Ah," said Uncle Joe. "Tell me your dreams. In the end, the interpretation of dreams is something that belongs to God. But perhaps I can be God's servant and yours in this matter. Tell me your dreams."

The chief cupbearer said, "In my dream I saw a vine. On the vine there were three branches. Right before my eyes I saw the vine begin to bud; then it blossomed, and then the clusters ripened into grapes. Pharoah's cup was in my hand; and I pressed the grapes and filled the cup, and handed the cup to the Pharoah."

Uncle Joe nodded, and said, "Yes. The interpretation is this. The three branches are three days. Within three days Pharoah will lift up your head and restore you to your office, and you will once more be chief cupbearer to the king, placing the cup in Pharoah's hand."

The chief cupbearer and the chief baker looked at each other. This was good news indeed. They nodded to Uncle Joe.

He bowed in return, and then he said this. "I do have one request. When you are restored to your office, remember me. Please do me the kindness to mention my case to Pharoah; for I was sold unjustly into slavery in my own country, and have done nothing to deserve being thrown into prison for all these years."

The chief baker liked what Uncle Joe had said to the chief cupbearer, and so now he said, "Here is my dream. I was carrying a stack of three baskets of cakes on my head. In the top basket there were all kinds of baked goods for Pharoah to eat. The birds of the air were landing on the basket and eating the food."

Uncle Joe nodded, and said, "Yes. The interpretation is this. The three baskets are three days. Within three days Pharoah will lift up your head—from you!—and hang you on a pole; and the birds will come and eat the flesh from you."

And on the third day after that, both of these things happened. Pharoah lifted up the head of the chief cupbearer, and restored him to office; and Pharoah lifted up the head of the chief baker, and hanged him.

The chief cupbearer was so glad to be back in his old position once more. Those anxious days in prison were best forgotten, he told himself, and so he forgot them. And he forgot about Uncle Joe, too.

And two more years passed. Uncle Joe had turned 30. For a long time he had known that he could end up living in this dungeon for the rest of his life. For a long time he had hoped that he might get out; and then for a longer time he had been afraid to hope that this could ever change. Then he had listened to the dreams of the chief cupbearer and the chief baker, and had known what they meant. And then the chief cupbearer was released from prison and went back to his job in the court of the king. And Uncle Joe did not dare to hope, Uncle Joe had resolved that he would not hope; but in spite of his decision, he found that he *had* hoped. He had hoped that the chief cupbearer would remember him, he had hoped that the chief cupbearer might mention his case; and Uncle Joe had hoped he would get a chance to defend himself and prove his innocence and be set free. But by now it was pretty obvious that these hopes were in vain; it was useless to hope; none of this was ever going to happen; he would live out the rest of his days there in the dungeon.

But it was then that Pharoah himself was troubled by dreams in the night. In his dream he saw seven cows, sleek and robust and full of health; the seven finest blue-ribbon cows anyone has ever seen. Then came seven more cows, bony and malnourished; the seven ugliest cows you could ever imagine. Cows eat grass and grain; they do not eat meat, and they certainly do not eat other cows. But in this dream, the scrawny cows gobbled up the healthy ones, meat and bones, hoofs and tails, so that nothing was left over; and when they were done, they still looked just as famished as ever.

Pharoah awoke, full of astonishment at such a dream. And he fell asleep again, and dreamed. In his dream this time he saw a stalk of corn, proud and strong, with seven ears growing on it, plump and full of kernels; and then seven more ears appeared, empty and blighted; and the seven thin ears consumed the seven full ones.

In the morning Pharoah called together his advisors, and asked them what these dreams foretold. But there was no one who could say.

Then the chief cupbearer said, "My lord Pharoah, I remember something. I should have remembered it sooner. Two years ago there was an incident that displeased you, and it appeared at the time that both the chief baker and I were at fault. You had us put in the dungeon. There we met a prisoner, a foreigner, who is skilled in the interpretation of dreams. The baker and I each dreamed a dream, and he told us the meaning. He explained that I would be restored to office, and the baker would be hanged. His interpretation was correct; for three days later, that is what my lord Pharoah ruled."

When Pharoah heard this, he sent for Uncle Joe to be brought from the dungeon. Well, first they made sure that Uncle Joe took a bath and got shaved and put on clean clothes. And when Uncle Joe stood before him, Pharoah said to him, "I have heard that you are a skilled interpreter of dreams. I have dreamed a pair of dreams, and they trouble my soul, and I need to know what they mean."

Uncle Joe said, "It is not really me. God is the one who gives insights. But tell me your dreams, sir, and I will listen to you and to God and see what I can say."

Pharoah told his story, about the seven fat cows and the seven scrawny cows, and about the seven plump ears and the seven blighted ears.

Uncle Joe nodded, and said, "Yes. The interpretation is this. The two dreams are one: they both mean the same thing. The seven fat cows are seven years, and the seven scrawny cows are seven years: it means seven years of plenty for the land of Egypt, followed by seven years of famine. The seven plump ears are seven years, and the seven blighted ears are seven years: it confirms the first dream, for it also means seven years of plenty for the land of Egypt, followed by seven years of famine. God has shown Pharoah what is about to happen. There will be seven years of bumper crops, of great abundance. And then will come seven years of severe famine, such as has never been known."

Pharoah and all his advisors were greatly troubled by this. Seven years of famine would destroy the nation.

Then Uncle Joe said this. "Here is what Pharoah should do. Pharoah should appoint someone to be overseer over all the production of the land, with officers to report to this overseer. During the seven years of plenty that are coming, Pharoah should claim one fifth of all the production of the land, and store it away in granaries. Let that be for a reserve, to feed the people during the seven years of famine, to keep them alive."

This proposal pleased Pharoah and his court. Pharoah said, "Since the spirit of God is so clearly with this man, to give him such discernment and wisdom, he is the man we want to be in charge of this." And so Pharoah appointed Uncle Joe to be the Prime Minister of Egypt. He set him in charge of all the production, in charge of taxes, in charge of all the granaries.

And thus, when he was thirty years old, and after twelve long years in the dungeon, Uncle Joe's life changed completely all in one single day. When he woke up he was just another forgotten prisoner; but by nightfall he had had a bath, met the king, and become Prime Minister of Egypt.

The seven years of plenty came to pass, right on schedule. There was grumbling, of course, about the amount of grain that the government confiscated and stored away. A farmer's lot is never easy, and many years it feels like you are just getting by; then when a bumper-crop year finally happens, you want to sell all that extra grain and make your very best profits ever. Still, even after a fifth of the crop had been claimed by the tax officers, there was food for everyone in the land, and plenty left over to ship to other nations.

By the fourth year, every barn and granary throughout the land of Egypt was full. Well, every barn and granary that had existed before the king's dream. Uncle Joe had foreseen this, however, and had organized and built new granaries in every city, and these new granaries continued to receive one fifth of all the production of the land. By the end of the seventh year they had stored away an amazing amount of grain.

Then began the years of famine. The first year was harsh and dry, the way the first year of a drought often is. Most everyone was prepared for it, though. People had long since learned that a year with not enough rain could lead to starvation, and so every family tried very hard to keep extra grain stored in their own pantries and storage sheds, in large clay jars with snug lids to keep the insects and mice out, so that they could keep going even during a lean year. It was the second year of drought when it really began to pinch. By the third year, people were hurting badly. If it had not been for Uncle Joe and the food that he had put by for the whole nation, all the people of Egypt would have starved.

Not just the people of Egypt, either. The people of Libya and Ethiopia, the people of Arabia and Canaan and Assyria, the people of Babylon and Persia: there was deep famine in so many regions, among so many families. The people of these lands heard that there was grain in Egypt, and they sent caravans to buy it. It was expensive. Yet the people of these nations paid the price, costly as it was; and the treasury of Egypt filled up with gold.

In the land of Canaan, Uncle Jacob said to his ten older sons, "You must go to Egypt and buy grain, to keep the family from starving." And so they packed up supplies and money, and took the road south from Canaan to Egypt.

When they got to Egypt, Uncle Joe recognized them. But they did not recognize him; and indeed how could they? They had not seen him for more than twenty years, and for all they knew he was dead, or working in a mine or on a farm hundreds of miles away from the capital, or long since sold to someone in another country. They bowed before the Prime Minister, this man about forty years old dressed in courtly Egyptian robes, this man issuing rapid-fire orders in the Egyptian language to various officers and messengers; there was no way that they could see in him their teenage kid brother from so many years ago.

But when one of the court officers had ushered in these ten brothers who had come from the land of Canaan, Uncle Joe had recognized them at once. He was careful not to react right away. Instead, he pondered on the meaning of this moment. There they were, his ten brothers who had sold him into slavery, bowing before him in humility, and stammering out in broken Egyptian words and phrases that they wished to buy grain. And Uncle Joe remembered the dream he had dreamed, back when he was that teenage kid brother: his dream that someday they would bow in recognition of his authority.

There was irony here. And vengeance, perhaps. Uncle Joe considered the possibilities. What did he wish to say to these brothers of his, who had sold him into slavery and now knelt in obeisance before him?

Uncle Joe signaled to his chief steward, a man gifted with languages. This man often translated for traders from Crete, Babylon, Assyria, and Phoenicia. Because the chief steward was interested in the tongues of various nations, Uncle Joe had taught him a fair amount of his own dialect, from his home in Canaan. And so the chief steward stepped forward to greet these foreign traders. From their appearance he guessed they might be Phoenician, and offered them peace and welcome in that language. They stammered and stumbled in their efforts to reply, and in their comments to one another about this language difficulty the steward recognized the Canaanite dialect he had learned from his master, the Prime Minister. He looked back at Uncle Joe, seated there looking attentive but otherwise giving no sign that he understood; and so the chief steward took his cue from that. He began to address the brothers in their own Canaanite dialect. They were surprised and grateful to discover that someone here in Egypt could speak in their own language, and asked the chief steward how it was that he could do that. He replied, modestly, that this was his assigned task, to interpret for various foreign dignitaries and traders who came to the Egyptian court. "We are all in the hands of God," he said, "who gives such abilities to one individual or another, and then expects us to use them well. I am honored to be able to be of use in your service, as you come to trade here." This did not answer their question, of course, but it was still a fine example of courtesy, and so with the chief steward translating for them, they explained where they were from, and said that they wished to buy grain to feed their family.

Uncle Joe replied, in Egyptian, "Clearly you are spies. You have come to cause trouble in our land."

When the chief steward translated that for them, they protested their innocence, of course. They insisted that they were simply a large family; they were twelve sons of one father, though one son had died long ago and the youngest had stayed at home with their father back in Canaan; in the midst of this famine they had come for no other reason than to buy grain. Uncle Joe listened as the steward translated this explanation, but only for a moment. He said again, "Clearly you are spies."

Then he signaled to the guards, and the ten brothers were thrown into prison.

After three days he had the ten brothers brought to him once again. "Here is how I will test you, to see if you are telling the truth. One of you will stay here as a hostage; the others can purchase grain and take it back to feed your families in Canaan. When you come back again, you must bring your younger brother with you, to prove that your story is true; otherwise, I will know that you are indeed spies."

The ten brothers listened as the chief steward explained all this, and then they nodded in agreement—for what choice did they have? Yet even while they accepted this condition, they fretted among themselves. "This is the hand of God," they said. "God is paying us back for the evil we did all those years ago. We sold a brother into slavery in Egypt; now we are forced to leave a brother as hostage in Egypt." They spoke rapidly and in slang among themselves, to make sure that the chief steward could not follow what they said; but Uncle Joe understood every word. And Uncle Reuben said, "Why would none of you listen to me, when I said we should not harm the lad? Now indeed we face a reckoning for his blood."

Uncle Joe was suddenly overcome with emotion. He stepped aside, and felt the tears pour from his eyes: though he could not quite name what the emotion was that he felt so strongly, in that moment. Was it gladness at seeing them squirm? Sorrow over lost years? Mercy? Vindication? He could not tell. Just that his heart and eyes were flooding with—something. Something very powerful.

Somehow he composed himself once again, and turned back to confront the brothers. He pointed to one—it was Uncle Simeon, as it turns out—and commanded that he be put in chains. The other nine brothers watched in horror as the guards fastened iron fetters around Uncle Simeon's wrists, and wrapped a chain around his waist and ran the end of the chain through the fetters. Then Uncle Joe commanded that the nine brothers could buy as much grain as their donkeys could carry.

The guards led Uncle Simeon back to the prison, and the chief steward led the other nine brothers out to one of the granaries, to sell them sacks of grain. As they left the court, Uncle Joe nodded to himself as he reached a decision. He turned to one of his elite officers and gave him these orders: "After they finish purchasing their grain, gather up the specific coins that they use to buy it. Then, before they leave tomorrow morning, put each man's money back in his grain sack. Don't let anyone see you do it."

You can imagine the anxiety of the brothers, as they made their way back to Canaan, leaving Uncle Simeon behind. When they discovered that they still had their money—the very same coins that they had used to pay for the grain!—their anxiety increased tenfold. What could it mean? Was it a trap? Was it an accident? What they feared the most was that God could be doing something. God could be doing something to punish them for their sins, something even more severe than the punishment of leaving Simeon as hostage in Egypt.

They reached home with their load of grain. Our family was secure once more. All of us had enough to eat, for many months to come.

But Uncle Jacob was greatly troubled, when they recounted to him all that had happened to them in Egypt. "My son Joseph is no more," he lamented. "And on this trip you have lost my son Simeon, leaving him captive in the land of Egypt. And now you say that you should take my son Benjamin with you next time you go. Truly you will bereave me of all my children, and leave me as a broken old man, full of sorrow."

Sorrow or not, people have to eat. All of our people were skilled foragers and hunters, but in the midst of the great drought there was little to find. The rains did not fall, and the gardens did not grow. Much of the livestock had perished, and much of what remained was sickly. The family was cautious with the grain that the brothers had brought back from Egypt; they were frugal, even miserly, as they rationed it out to make it last many months, until the rains came at last to water the earth and bring forth the crops for a new year. If the rains had come, they would have succeeded. But the rains did not come. The heavens were shut up, and the land remained parched and barren. And slowly the reserves dwindled. It became obvious that they would need to purchase more grain, or they would all die.

So Uncle Jacob gathered his sons together, and instructed them to go once again to Egypt, in order to buy food to keep the family alive.

"The prime minister accused us of being spies, my Father," said Uncle Judah. "He insisted that if we wish to prove that we are honest men, not spies from a foreign land but just brothers in a large hungry family, we must bring our brother Benjamin with us. That is the proof he demanded. If you are willing to send Benjamin with us, we will go and buy grain. But if not, there is no point in going. The man was very clear about this. We will not be able to buy food, unless we bring Benjamin with us."

"Why do you all hate me so much?" cried Uncle Jacob. "Have some pity for an old grey-haired man. Why did you even mention Benjamin to the man, and cause all this trouble?"

"The man questioned us in detail," the brothers answered. "He asked all kinds of questions about us, about you, about the family. How could we have known that he would pick up on this detail, and decide to use it this way? How could we have known what he would say?"

And then Uncle Judah said this. "I will stand surety for Benjamin. You can hold me accountable for him. If I fail to bring him back, let me bear the blame forever."

So Uncle Jacob agreed. He instructed them to bring choice gifts, and to take twice as much money: all the money from before, plus the same amount again to purchase new grain.

When they arrived in Egypt, Uncle Joe saw that they had brought another brother with them. It was Benjamin, all grown up. Little Benny had been just a boy of two when Uncle Joseph was sold into slavery, and now he was a fine young man in his mid-twenties. But the family resemblance was there, and Uncle Joe recognized him. So Uncle Joe instructed his chief steward, "Make arrangements for a big feast, for noon today. These men are to eat with me, in the great banquet hall of the Prime Minister's residence."

So the steward escorted the brothers to the house. That made them all nervous. They said to each other, "It's because of the money. Something is wrong about the way the money was returned to us, and he is setting this up so that he'll have a pretext to arrest us all and take everything we have." When they had talked it over among themselves, they said to the steward: "Sir, when we came to Egypt before to buy grain, we discovered on the way back home that all of our money had been restored to us; all of our coins were in the top of our grain sacks. So we have brought that money back with us, to restore it to you, along with additional money to purchase grain this time. But we affirm to you that we do not know how the money got put in our sacks, last time."

The chief steward shrugged. "I know that we received your money last time. So maybe your God worked a miracle and put treasure in your sacks last time, or something."

Just then the guards brought in Simeon, no longer in chains, looking a little frayed but otherwise all right. So the brothers took care of their donkeys, washed up and put on clean clothes; and on a large table they laid out all the gifts they had brought for the prime minister, to present to him when he came home for the feast at noon.

When Uncle Joe arrived, they all bowed to the ground before him. They presented him with the gifts from their father, Uncle Jacob. In rapid Egyptian Uncle Joe told the chief steward to ask them about the old man's health, and they replied that he was well. Uncle Joe looked at Benjamin, and asked them to introduce him. "God be gracious to you, son," he said to him. And as the chief steward was translating these words, Uncle Joe's heart blazed within him, flaring so hot he thought he just might burst into flames with the fiery emotions swirling in his soul. He hurried out of the room, down the hall to his own personal suite; and in the privacy of his own room he wept. Such a confusion of feelings: his little baby brother all grown up, and all his brothers bowing to the earth before him, just like the dream he had dreamed so many years ago. He felt the delicious possibility of making them squirm, and he felt the astonishing irony of this moment. He had not sobbed like this since he was a small boy, he thought. Finally the tears slowed, and then stopped. He washed his face and made himself presentable again, and then went back to the banquet hall.

During the feast Uncle Joe sat by himself at the great high table. This table was big enough for twenty people to eat together, but on this occasion only Uncle Joe was seated there. It was to his table that the cooks and the waiters brought all of the food. Several officers had the responsibility of tasting the food and the wine, to make sure that nothing was poisoned; and then the cooks and waiters took all the choicest parts and presented them to Uncle Joe, as prime minister. After he had made his selection, they would take from the food that he had not chosen for himself, and carry portions from that to serve the other tables.

While Uncle Joe sat all by himself at the high table, the officers of the court sat at the second table, and the eleven brothers sat at the last table. These two groups, the court officers and the brothers, had to keep separate from each other. It would have been difficult for them to chat around the table in any case, because of the difference in languages; but it was more than that. Each group considered that the other group's social class was far inferior to their own. When people ate at the same table, that said something very important: it said that they were friends and family with one another, it said that they had a mutual responsibility and relationship together, a covenant established by sharing food together at a common table. And that wasn't the kind of relationship that either group intended to have with the other.

As Uncle Joe looked around the room, he came to a decision. Ordinarily he would just choose the portions he wanted for himself and eat his meal, leaving it up to the cooks and waiters to take not-quite-the-best portions to the officers at the second table, and then to take plain-but-adequate portions to whatever unimportant people happened to have been seated at the low table for this particular meal. But Uncle Joe decided that he was going to do something out of the ordinary. He made specific assignments of portions to go to the table where all the brothers were seated. He made sure that all of them got lots of good things to eat. But he made sure that his baby brother, Uncle Benjamin, got the very best selection of all.

All the brothers were impressed and delighted with this hospitality, far more than they expected. Their hearts continued to be quite merry, after the banquet was over, as they arranged to buy the grain to take back home to their father, Uncle Jacob, and the rest of their families. But Uncle Joe was not finished with them. For he had again assigned special orders to the same elite officer as before: "Let these men purchase all the grain their animals can carry. When they have done that, collect up all the coins that they have used to make their purchases, and put each man's money back in his grain sack, just like before. But this time, I want you to do one more thing. Take my silver cup, and place it in the grain sack of the youngest of the brothers. Make sure no one sees you do any of this."

So the brothers left, early the next morning. They had traveled for only a couple of hours when a squadron of soldiers came riding up behind them and made them stop. The chief steward was in charge, and he said to the brothers, "What is this that you have done? You have stolen the Prime Minister's silver cup! How can you do such a thing, to return evil for the good that he has done to you!"

They denied it, of course. "We even brought back the money that appeared in our sacks, from the last journey! We have no desire to steal; we are honest men who only came to buy food. Search all of our belongings, and you will see that none of us have stolen anything; but if you find that someone has done so, let him be put to death, and the rest of us will become your slaves."

The steward nodded his head. "As you say: if the cup is found among you, the one who has it will become my slave, and the others will be free to go."

So one by one, each man's baggage was searched, beginning with the eldest, Uncle Reuben. All of them were quite surprised to find their money in their sacks, once again; but the steward just shrugged over this, as he had before. Then the last grain sack was opened, and there was the cup: in the sack of Uncle Benjamin.

Uncle Benjamin shrieked, "I didn't do it!" But of course that didn't matter at all. The soldiers seized him, bound his hands behind his back, put him on his donkey, and brought him back to the city. And all the brothers loaded their grain and their baggage on their own donkeys once again, and rode back into the city as well, arguing with each other as they went. Had Benjamin stolen the cup? None of them could see how he would have had any opportunity to do that. During the meal, the silver cup had been on the Prime Minister's table, and Benjamin had never gotten close to it. During the night, they had all been together in one common room; Benjamin could hardly have gone sneaking around looking for things to steal without anyone noticing. But then, how had the cup—and all the money—gotten into their grain sacks once more?

When they came to Uncle Joe's house once again, they knelt before him with their faces to the ground. Uncle Joe spoke to them in a scornful voice: "What is this transgression that you have committed? Did you think that I would not be able to perceive your crime?" The brothers did not understand the words, but the disdain was utterly clear.

As they listened to the chief steward's translation, none of them knew what to say. What reply could they possibly make? All they could feel was the weight of disaster, pressing them into the earth.

Finally Uncle Judah spoke up. He offered no defense. Truly Benjamin was innocent, but Uncle Judah made no effort to argue that. His plea was simple: he pleaded for the life of his father, Uncle Jacob. He explained how he had promised his father to stand surety for Benjamin, because his father's life was tied up with the life of this youngest son. It would kill the old man, if Benjamin did not return. "And so this is the plea I make, sir," said Uncle Judah. "I ask that you please take me as your slave instead, for the sake of my father."

It was at this moment that Uncle Joe felt his heart overcome with emotion. He turned to the court officers standing nearby and said, "Leave me alone with these men." And so the chief steward and the other officials left the room. And Uncle Joe said, "I am your brother Joseph. Tell me, is our father indeed still alive?" And he burst into tears as he said it.

The brothers were stunned. They could not say a word, filled with shock as they recognized that it really was their brother Joseph—and filled with fear for what he might do to them.

"Stand up," Uncle Joe told them. "Come here, closer to me." And as they got to their feet and moved closer, he said, "I am your brother Joseph, whom you sold into slavery. And yet see what God has done, bringing me here ahead of the rest of you, to preserve the life of the family. The drought and the famine have been afflicting the land for more than two years, and there are almost five years to go before years of plenty will come again. God sent me before you, in order to keep the family alive. And now here is what you must do. Go back to our father, and tell him that I am here; and tell him that he and all the family must come here to Egypt, where I will make sure you have food to eat, and land where the cattle can graze."

Slowly the truth sank in: but even as it all came clear, the brothers still could hardly believe it. Their brother had become Prime Minister of Egypt! He controlled the wealth of a nation, and he could keep the family alive! But—how much vengeance might he yet take? That question would remain as an unanswered anxiety in their souls: but for now, here he was, hugging them all, kissing them, holding them with fierce hugs and hot tears.

Soon the brothers were on their way, with the donkeys pulling carts that Pharoah himself had provided, in order to carry all the family, young and old, back to the land of Egypt. Old Uncle Jacob was astonished, when he learned that his beloved son Joseph was still alive and well—and not only still alive, but ruling over all the land of Egypt. They tried to explain all that had happened, but Uncle Jacob would not listen. "Enough talk!" he said. "Get things loaded up. My son Joseph is still alive. Now I must go to see him before I die." So all the family moved to Egypt: Jacob and his three wives who were still living, his eleven sons and their wives, more than forty grandchildren, plus great-grandchildren, servants and retainers.

And the family prospered, there in the land of Egypt, with good land where the cattle could graze, and plenty to eat, even during the remaining years of the drought. Uncle Jacob had become quite an old man, and he was held in honor by all. And when he died, full of wisdom and shrewdness to the end, his family mourned. They told stories about his life, and they remembered the things he had done and said. They wept with their loss. And yet they felt the power of those tears, paying honor to the patriarch of their clan, whose life had become part of their identity.

It came to pass, however, that the ten brothers felt the anxiety growing in them once again. "Perhaps Joseph has just been biding his time," they told each other, "not wanting to wreak his vengeance on us while our father was still alive."

So they concocted a story. They met with Uncle Joe, and they told him this: "About a week before he died," they said, "our father expressed to us a last request. You were busy with Prime Minister business that day, and so you were not there. He told us to tell you not to hold a grudge against us, for his sake."

And Uncle Joe smiled. "Here is what I have come to understand," he said. "It is something that you must understand as well. You did this thing, intentionally, knowing it was bad; but God used it for good."

This is one of the deepest truths of our family. It is one of the stories we all should know: you should learn this, my child, and you should tell it to your children and your grandchildren. "You meant it for evil, but God used it for good." This is the capstone of this story that tells us who we are, and who God is.

The story of our life is that we are people who do the things we do, not because we want to be good, but because we have decided to do what we want even though we know it is not right. We are the people who do things, intentionally, knowing that what we are doing is bad (although we are often slow to admit that). We are the people who do it, intentionally, knowing it is bad—that is, we sin—not because we didn't know any better, and not just by being clumsy, but because even though we know that what we want to do is wrong, we do it anyway.

We are the people who do bad things on purpose: not as if we want to be evil like a cartoon villain laughing with a wicked cackle of fiendish glee, but because we know what is right and what is wrong, and we choose to do what is wrong. We are the people who do something, intentionally, knowing it is bad: who then discover that God uses it for good. God uses it for good, working grace and redemption into our lives despite our sins.

"You did this thing, knowing it was bad," said Uncle Joe. "But God used it for good."

Mark it well, my nieces and nephews. This is our story. We are the ones who have sinned; we are the ones who have done our deeds, intentionally, knowing it was bad; but God moves in the midst of our deeds, and in the end—sometimes indeed over the course of many years—our gracious God brings to pass healing and goodness even through our worst deeds.

Well. That's how Uncle Joe became Prime Minister of Egypt. The time in Egypt was not always good for us; but in those days, when our family first got there, those were good days.

So now let me tell you how it was that Uncle Jacob's family got to be a family.

3

At Your Heels

People tell different stories about how Uncle Red got to be called Uncle Red. One way they tell it is, when he was born, he came out with a full head of red hair. Lots of babies are bald, of course, and some are born with just the finest, faintest hair, soft as soft can be: so soft that it has almost no color, and you can see right through it. And some babies have a lot of hair: which might be one color when they first arrive and then change into something different as they grow.

But one of the ways I heard it, Uncle Red had more hair than any baby you ever saw, not only on his head but some on the back of his neck and even some fuzz on his shoulders. It was a dark reddish color, and when they held him up in the light for his mama, Aunt Rebekah, to see for the first time, she said "Red!" Maybe she was just reacting to the color, rather than deliberately naming him at that moment; but once they got him dried off, that hair was even brighter red and the sunlight made it glow: and so Red it was. He never lost that hair, like babies sometimes do; even as a child he had hair on his arms and forearms, and by the time he was a teenager he was downright shaggy. It made him look fierce. He liked it.

Back when he was first born, though, it turns out that it was twins. Aunt Rebekah had known it was twins, before anyone else knew. She had had a hard time getting pregnant, and Uncle Isaac had prayed for her; and then when God answered that prayer and she got pregnant, it became a very uncomfortable pregnancy. Along about the sixth month or so, when she didn't yet know it was twins, those two babies were bumping and kicking each other in the womb, and so they were kicking her as well, it seemed like all the time.

The men of the family have not always remembered this part of the story. The women have known. They have known that pregnancy and labor lead to childbirth and newness of life—except when they lead to death, which has always been tragically often. The aunts have always been aware of the mixture of the promise of life and the danger of death, and yet when the uncles tell the stories they sometimes forget some of these details. But there is this part of the family lore concerning Aunt Rebekah that the women have remembered and handed down from generation to generation.

They remember this peculiar line, from the midst of Aunt Rebekah's challenging pregnancy:

"She said, 'If it be thus, why do I live?' So she went to inquire of the Lord."

The aunts have remembered that Aunt Rebekah, in her weariness and frustration and pain, asked that question out loud: and then she reckoned that it wasn't enough, just to ask it out loud to see if the wind or the night sky would answer: she needed to present that kind of question directly to God.

"Is this the way my life, my death, is going to be? If so, what's the point of going on?" Sometimes people have that kind of question, and yet they never quite ask it out loud. Other times they ask it out loud, with fear or anger or sorrow, and yet they never quite ask it as a prayer. The family lore is clear on this, though. This is the story of Aunt Rebekah and God: it tells us how she asked, "if it be thus, why do I live?" And then she went to inquire of the Lord.

And it tells us how the Lord answered her.

"There are two nations in your womb," said God. "These two babies will become two peoples, and they will each go their own way. One will be stronger than the other: and the elder will serve the younger."

What could that mean? It would turn out to be a puzzle along the way. Which one would be stronger? Why would it be, that the elder would serve the younger? Aunt Rebekah did not quite know what to make of God's answer to her prayer. But she knew at least this much, before anyone else knew: she knew it was twins.

Usually twins are born a few minutes apart, but Uncle Jacob put in his appearance right on the heels of his brother. In fact, his little hand was kind of wrapped around the tiny baby heel of Red. So they named him Jacob, which means something like "at your heels."

It is an ambiguous name, because being behind someone is an ambiguous place to be. From behind you I can protect you, support you, keep anybody else from sneaking up on you. And from behind you I can ambush you, betray you, backstab you. What does it mean, if I am at your heels? Perhaps I can convince you to have confidence in me, because like the saying goes in our present era, "I've got your back"—and as the saying went in another era, when Uncle Moses sang to our people as they prepared to cross the Jordan into the promised land: God's angels followed "at your heels" to guard you along the way. But perhaps, instead, "at your heels" will mean trouble for you: one day I will be hiding in the tall grass, and when you come down the path I will suddenly leap from behind you and tackle your ankles and throw you to the ground.

I've always thought that it must have been interesting for Uncle Jacob, growing up with a name like "At Your Heels," with all its ambiguity.

Uncle Red grew up to be an outdoorsman, running races, learning to hunt and fish. Uncle Jacob was more of a stay-at-home kind of boy, quiet and reflective. Parents are supposed to love their children equally, but as you know it doesn't always happen that way. Uncle Isaac loved his boy Red, for his brash personality and his skill in the outdoors, and because he loved the wild game that the young hunter would bring home, which would get slow-cooked in the stew pot into a wonderful delicious burgoo. But Aunt Rebekah knew what God had told her about how in the end the elder would serve the younger. She did not see how that would happen: it seemed obvious enough that the first born, Red, would end up with his father's blessing, and the younger would end up serving him. Still, Aunt Rebekah remembered what God had said. And she believed it: and she loved her boy Jacob.

There was this one time, I guess the boys were about 12 or 14 or so. Uncle Red had been out hunting all day long, and had had no luck at all. He got home with the ravenous hunger of a teenage boy, sure that he would starve to death in the next few minutes if he didn't get something to eat. In the meantime, Uncle Jacob had been cooking that afternoon. Uncle Red often made fun of Uncle Jacob for being a sissy—you know how adolescents can tease and mock each other—but he didn't call him a sissy this time, because Uncle Jacob had made chili—Red Lentil Chili—and the aroma was powerful and rich and full of flavor.

"Wow, that smells great," said Uncle Red. "Give me some of that red stuff you've got there." (That reminds me, there's actually another branch of the family lore that says he got the name Red because of this very story, and because he was always so fond of Red Lentil Chili.)

"Hmm, maybe I'll let you have some," said Uncle Jacob. "Dang, it sure smells good, doesn't it? I've been working on this new recipe, and I think I've got the blend of spices just about perfect. Really, though, I was thinking I should give this batch to Mom and Dad to try. But hey, there's still plenty of dried lentils left in that sack over there, so you can cook some up for yourself if you like. If you start right now, you could have another pot of chili finished in a couple of hours."

"No way," said Uncle Red. "I'm about to die, here. Let me have some of that."

"Tell you what I'm gonna do," said Uncle Jacob, looking very thoughtful. "You know you've got the birthright, since you were born a few moments before me. So how about we make a trade? If you're willing to swap with me for your birthright, I'll give you this whole pot of chili in exchange."

"Ha, sure. You can have the birthright, what do I need that for when I am about to starve. Just hurry up and give me a bowl of it, or get out of my way and I'll get it myself."

"Here you go," said Uncle Jacob, as he started to hand over the bowl of chili—and then he pulled it back for a moment. "You swear, right? You have to swear it: that you trade your birthright for my Red Lentil Chili."

Uncle Red said "Yeah, yeah, I swear. You dork." And he reached across and snatched the bowl, and commenced to serious eating.

And Uncle Jacob—Uncle At-Your-Heels—just smiled. And then, as he saw Uncle Red making his way rapidly through that bowl of chili, he turned back to the pot and smiled some more as he ladled out a second bowl for Uncle Red.

Time marches on. The boys reached the fullness of adulthood: here they were, grown up men. Uncle Red got married. In fact, he got himself double married, with two wives: Judith and Basemath. And then, as it turns out, these two wives began to make fun of Uncle Isaac and Aunt Rebekah.

It is a critical part of our identity that all down the ages we have been this great extensive clan, all down the ages; but a major factor in our family story is that even though we are one big family, we have not always succeeded in being one big happy family. There was strife in those days, strife between Uncle Red's wives and his parents. I do not know what it was that motivated Aunt Judith and Aunt Basemath to make fun of Uncle Isaac and Aunt Rebekah. Perhaps they had come to an intuitive agreement: it would be uncomfortable if they spent their lives sniping at each other as rival wives each trying to be the favored one, and so they would take out their frustrations by seeing Uncle Isaac and Aunt Rebekah as the common target of their sniping.

Or perhaps they had simply decided to make fun of the ever-more-noticeable difference in age between Uncle Isaac and Aunt Rebekah. Uncle Isaac had been a man in his prime when he had married Aunt Rebekah, and she had been a mere slip of a girl at the time, about 25 years younger than he was. Now he was rapidly becoming an old man; and while no one would mistake Aunt Rebekah for a teenager any more, she was still vibrant and healthy and a fine figure of a woman. Perhaps it was the sight of Uncle Isaac—an old man whose eyes were failing and whose health was becoming increasingly frail, cared for by a wife still strong and pretty—that led these two wives, themselves still in their teens, to mock Uncle Isaac and Aunt Rebekah. I do not know if it was this. Perhaps it was something else. The family annals do not specify. Only that there was something, sly under-the-breath comments or open insolence, that greatly aggravated Aunt Rebekah and Uncle Isaac.

The day came when Uncle Isaac felt the sureness in his soul that he was not long for this world. He was not quite blind, but his eyes had dimmed to the point where he could not see much more than the difference between daylight and the dark of night. He had become nearly bedfast. And so he called for Uncle Red. Uncle Isaac didn't like Uncle Red's wives, but Red was still his son—still the son that he loved the best—and he wanted to give him his official blessing.

When Uncle Red came up to Uncle Isaac's bedside, Uncle Isaac told him, "I am an old man. My days are numbered, and from the weary ache I feel in my bones, I think the number is not large. So I have a last request for you: go hunt me some wild game, and prepare a nice burgoo. I just love the way the flavors of different kinds of wild game all blend together in a fine burgoo, and I want to have one more dish of burgoo before I die. Do this, my son, and you will have my blessing."

Aunt Rebekah was down at the other end of the tent while this conversation was going on, busy with some housework. Neither Uncle Red nor Uncle Isaac was paying any attention to her, and so they did not realize that she was paying attention to them. Uncle Red went out and got his hunting gear together, and headed out to the fields to see what game he might find, to make the best burgoo there ever was. And Aunt Rebekah sat for a moment and pondered.

She recalled the word that had come to her, when she had despaired of life during the hard days of her pregnancy, and had gone to inquire of the Lord. That word had said that one of her sons would be stronger. Which of her sons would that be? Jacob had always been her favorite, but was he also the strongest? Maybe he was: not strong in hunting or in running, perhaps, but maybe strong in perception and in shrewdness. Maybe that was the strength that would make the most difference, where things really counted. Except that it apparently was not going to do that, for here was her husband getting ready to give his blessing to his older son, despite what God had said on the day of her desperate prayers, all those years ago, when God said, "The elder will serve the younger."

Unless—

Aunt Rebekah got up and quietly moved out of the tent, and found Uncle Jacob. "Go at once and choose the best two yearling goats, and kill them and bring them to me. Your father has sent your brother out to hunt for wild game, to make burgoo; and then he intends to give your brother his blessing. But if we hurry, we can accomplish everything before he gets back."

Uncle Jacob hesitated. Not because he was too noble to try to trick his father this way, but because it seemed so unlikely that he could get away with it. "Father may be blind, but he can still tell his two sons apart," he said. "Even if he doesn't know it's me just from my voice, he'll surely reach out his hand and touch me on the arm, and right away he'll know whether it is me, or Red with his shaggy red hair all over his forearms and all."

"You leave that to me," said Aunt Rebekah, "and go fetch me those goats." So that's what Uncle Jacob did. She instructed Uncle Jacob to cut up the meat and put it in the kettle over the fire. Soon the rich meat aroma was beginning to fill the air as the broth bubbled merrily in the stewpot. In the meantime, Aunt Rebekah took the hide from the leg quarters of one of the goats. She cut and shaped the leather into two extra-long bracers, long enough to stretch from Uncle Jacob's elbows down to his wrists, with an extra tab that covered the backs of his hands. She punched holes along the edges and threaded rawhide laces through those holes, and then she fitted the finished pieces around Uncle Jacob's forearms. When she had laced them up, there he was, with big shaggy forearms, just like his brother, Uncle Red. She cut another piece of goatskin and fashioned it into a broad collar the same way. Uncle Jacob thought they looked bad and smelled worse, but Aunt Rebekah said they'd work just fine.

Then she turned her attention to the burgoo. The meat had gotten nice and tender in the stewpot, and the broth was rich and brown. She added some lentils, some cumin and some salt, some garlic and some turnips, to make the savory blend just the way her husband Uncle Isaac had always liked it best.

When the burgoo was done, Aunt Rebekah mixed up some pancake batter, and fried up half a dozen pancakes on a griddle over the coals. Then she said, "Now is the time. Get that shirt off, and put on your brother's shirt. Hurry up."

"I just don't think this is going to work," said Uncle Jacob, taking off his shirt and pulling Uncle Red's shirt on over the collar and bracers of goat skin.

But Aunt Rebekah was putting a bowl onto a tray, and ladling into it a hearty serving of the burgoo. She added the plate of pancakes, and then she handed the tray to Uncle Jacob and sent him in to feed his father. And so he went.

Uncle Isaac was lying in his bed, dozing. Uncle Jacob set the tray down on the table, and came over toward the bedside and said, "Here I am, father."

Uncle Isaac tried to see something other than a vague shadow, but he could not. His voice was old and whispery as he asked, "Who is it, then?"

Bold as brass, Uncle Jacob smiled as he lied: "Why, it's me, Red, your first-born son. I did just what you asked me, father. Can you sit up a little? I've got a burgoo here, made of wild game, just the way you like it best."

"How did you find game so quickly?" asked Uncle Isaac. "I kind of thought you'd have to travel out quite a ways. We've hunted the nearby game just about down to nothing."

"The Lord your God granted me success," answered Uncle Jacob. "I had thought the same as you, that it would take me much longer; but I picked up the fresh tracks of a wild goat just at the edge of the hills, and the wind was right for me to be able to stalk it without it scenting me, and one shot was all it took."

Uncle Isaac had this uneasy sense that something wasn't quite right. Although the twins never looked much alike, their voices had always been quite similar, and sometimes at night when they were growing up, when you would call one of them the other one would answer, just to make a joke. There were a couple of the servants that would get fooled by that most every time. But Uncle Isaac was pretty sure he had never been fooled when they pulled that trick. Now that he had nearly gone blind, he had counted on his sense of hearing more than ever. And so it troubled him, because up to this moment he would have sworn that he could absolutely guarantee which one was which, as soon as he heard either of them speak a few words. But here he was, having a conversation with Red about hunting, and yet he if he didn't know better he would have said it was Jacob's voice.

Lying there on the bed, Uncle Isaac raised his hand and reached out to his son. This was the moment Uncle Jacob was dreading, but there was no way he could avoid it: he reached forward and brought his arm up underneath his father's hand. His father's grip, which had always been so full of strength, had grown feeble. Yet as Uncle Isaac's hand grasped Uncle Jacob's wrist, feeling the shaggy texture of the goatskin against his frail wrinkled palm, he said, "Bless you, my son. It really is you, isn't it, Red?" It was almost a statement, and yet in his frail reedy voice it held the edge of an uncertain question.

"Yes, it's me," said Uncle Jacob.

And Uncle Isaac said to himself, *I can't tell their voices apart any more.* He felt anew the pang of loss: he could no longer count on his eyes, and now it appeared that he could no longer count on his ears. *You are an old man, and getting older every day,* he said to himself. *Your vision is gone and your hearing is going; there is no strength left in your hands and even your voice has no more vigor than dead grass. You can smell the burgoo and taste it, but how long till those senses are gone as well? Soon you will be dead, old man. Better enjoy the burgoo while you still can, and pass on the blessing without any further delay.*

"All right, then," said Uncle Isaac, "let's try some of this burgoo."

And so Uncle Jacob brought the serving tray over and set it on the bed, and his father Uncle Isaac ate the bowl of burgoo and two of the pancakes, and drank a few sips of wine.

Then he said, "Kiss me, my son." And Uncle Jacob leaned in close, and kissed his father, first on one cheek, and then on the other. Uncle Isaac got a good whiff of Uncle Red's shirt, and recognized the smell of it. *All right,* he said to himself. *I can't see, and I can't tell their voices apart any longer, but I can still tell the difference by smell.*

And Uncle Isaac lifted up his hand, and placed it on Uncle Jacob's head; and as he began to speak the weariness of the years fell away, and his voice rang with the power of the word as he declared the blessing of God with resolute sureness. This is what he said, as he poured out his heart in the best blessing from father to son he could offer: "May God grant you the earth's richness, my son, with abundance of grain and sparkling new wine! May God establish you as the ruler of nations, and as the ruler of this family in the coming generations! May God requite everyone in accordance to their response to you: curses on those who curse you, blessings on those who bless you!"

It was a powerful blessing indeed, and Uncle Jacob thanked his father for it. And then he scooted out the door. He had done it!

And just in the nick of time, for Uncle Red was striding up to the household in the dusk, with a couple of rabbits and three pigeons strung on a line across his shoulders. He filled a kettle with water and cut up the meat into chunks and put them into the pot, and soon the water was bubbling as he cooked them into a burgoo. And when the meat was cooked through, he ladled it up into a bowl and brought it to his father.

"Here I am, father," he said. "I have brought you the burgoo you asked for. Can you sit up and eat some of it?"

"Who are you?" asked Uncle Isaac.

"Why, I'm Red, your first-born son," said Uncle Red. "You sent me out to hunt game for a burgoo, and I've done just what you said."

Uncle Isaac trembled; he felt the shaking in his arms and in his stomach, and all the way down to the very depths of his soul. This was indeed Red, by the voice. "Who then was here just a moment ago, serving me burgoo and receiving my blessing: the blessing that I have poured out on him with all my heart!"

"No!" cried Uncle Red, with a wail of heartbreak and bitter dismay. "Don't tell me you gave your blessing to Jacob! Don't give it all to him! Bless me, too, father!"

"Your brother has now received the blessing. I have given it to him, and so he has it."

Uncle Red said, "He has lived up to his name, for sure. 'At your heels'—he snuck up on me and tricked me about the birthright, and now he has snuck up on me and tricked me about the blessing." And a great hatred burned in Uncle Red's soul, at that moment.

And then he asked once again, "Haven't you reserved any blessing for me?"

Uncle Isaac had indeed intended to offer something to his second born: a secondary blessing for the secondary son, a blessing that probably would not have felt like that much of a blessing to Uncle Jacob, and certainly did not seem like one to Uncle Red: to serve his brother, to eke out some adequate living for himself as secondary brother while giving his best strength to the service of the primary brother, the one who had received the real blessing. Yet that was the 'blessing' that Uncle Isaac bestowed on Uncle Red: he would henceforth be the secondary son, and therefore it would be his 'blessing' to live his life in service to his brother.

Uncle Red had never in his life been cast into the role of secondary son. He did not like it; but that was the way it was. "I will be the second son now," he said, "and all the blessing and all the inheritance and all the power will belong to my brother, as long as he lives; and then to his children after him."

Unless—

—unless Jacob were to die before he had any children. Uncle Red thought long about that, as he stood out in the darkness, away from the tents, for a long time that night, feeling the darkness of the night and the darkness of his soul. He whispered into the wind, "Soon my father will be dead and gone. And I will mourn you, my father, for you have been a good man these many years. And when you are in your grave, it will not be long before this usurper is right at your heels: he will follow you to the grave, and very soon."

Uncle Red might have managed to pull off his planned murder, except that he was a mumbler. One of the servants overheard him a few days later, murmuring his threats under his breath, while he was watching Uncle Jacob carry a bucket of corn out to feed the two best calves, which were kept in a corral nearby instead of wandering with the rest of the herd. "The day is coming," he muttered, "when you're going to feel my knife slipping between your ribs. From behind. Because once Dad is dead, it will be my turn to come sneaking up on you, Mr. At-Your-Heels."

The servant brought the report to Aunt Rebekah. She thanked him. And then she went to talk to Uncle Isaac, who had not died quite as quickly as he had expected. "I have just had it up to here with those two little brats that Red has married," she said. "You know how they are."

Uncle Isaac nodded. He knew.

"I tell you what, honey, I don't want Jacob to pick up a miserable wife like that. What we should do is send him away, to my kinfolk, where they can fix him up with a wife who will be properly respectful."

Uncle Isaac said, "That's a good idea. I hate the way those girls are always giggling behind their hands. I can tell they are making fun of me, but I can never tell what exactly they are saying."

So Uncle Isaac called in his son Jacob and said, "Your mother and I have decided to send you away to her family, to get you a wife. You have an Uncle Laban that you need to talk to; I'm sure he'll fix you up." And the next morning, Uncle Jacob got up early, picked up his traveling bag, and headed off.

Uncle Red watched him walking away, in the early dawn. "Maybe he'll get eaten by a bear, while he is traveling through the wilderness," he thought. "Or he could get killed by bandits. Or maybe he'll get lost, and fall in a hole and break his leg and starve, in slow agony. That would be good, I like that one. Or maybe he'll just stay far away, with Uncle Laban's family, forever. Whatever. As long as he's not here, I'll be the number one son."

It took a couple of weeks of steady hiking for Uncle Jacob to make his way to Uncle Laban's home. There was this one night along the way, when he laid his blanket on the ground on top of a rocky hill. He had a small backpack that he carried, and usually he used this pack as his pillow when he went to sleep at each night's campsite. But on this particular night his feet felt so sore, weary and blistered and battered, and so as he lay down he propped his feet on top of his pack to elevate them and maybe make them feel a little better. There was a long slab of rock right at the edge of the blanket, and it was just in the right location so that Uncle Jacob ended up resting his head on this rock as if it were a pillow. As he lay there like that, it occurred to him that it would make more sense to pivot around and put his feet up on the rock and his head on the pack, but he was weary down to the depths and it seemed like too much effort. "What is this all about?" he asked himself. "I'm supposed to be the favored son now, with the birthright and the blessing, and yet here I am walking my feet off and so tired I can't even turn around." And with that he fell asleep.

That night Uncle Jacob had a dream. In his dream he saw a vision of heaven, with a great staircase between the earth and the sky, and he saw the angels of God ascending and descending the staircase, on their way back from doing the business of the Lord, or on their way out on new assignments. He had never seen an angel before, but right away he knew what they were. And then right away he stopped looking at the angels and the staircase, because even higher up, above the staircase, he saw God.

And God said, "I am the Lord, the God of your father Abraham and of your father Isaac. I am going to give you and your descendants this land on which you are sleeping right now! And your descendants will be so many, more than anyone can count, more than all the grains of dust in all the earth." And God went on speaking, and made this promise: "All the nations across the face of the earth will be blessed through you and your offspring, and I will be with you to watch over you, and I will bring you back to this very land. I will not fail to fulfill this promise."

Uncle Jacob had never had a dream like this before. Usually when you wake up from a dream, no matter how vivid or scary it was, no matter how hard your heart is hammering, you still know right away that it wasn't real: it was only a dream. But as Uncle Jacob woke up, he knew that this dream was the most real thing that he had ever experienced. "This was the very presence of God," he said to himself, trembling. "Surely the presence of the Lord is here, and I did not know it." But now Uncle Jacob did know it. And somehow he knew that this would be a defining moment for him: from here on his whole life would be lived in the awareness that in this one moment of vision and clarity, he had known for certain that he was in the presence of God.

In the dawn's early light Uncle Jacob got to work. He dug around the oblong slab of rock that had served as his pillow, until he could pry it loose from the ground; then he set it up on end for a makeshift altar, digging around the bottom so that the slab settled firmly into the earth. He brushed as much of the dirt off the top of the rock as he could; then he washed it with a couple splashes of water, and wiped it clean. He reached into his pack and pulled out a small clay jar of olive oil, wrapped in a scrap of cloth. He'd used up about half the jar, cooking his meals along the way. He wasn't sure if he had enough oil for the rest of the journey.

He didn't really know how much farther he had to go. But he shrugged, and poured a generous measure of the oil onto the top of the rock. "From now on," he said, "the name of this place will be Bethel, the house of God." And then he prayed, "If you will be with me, O God, to give me food to eat and clothes to wear on this journey, and if you will watch over me and bring me back safely to my father's house, then forever you will be my God, and forever this stone I have set up for an altar will be your house where I will worship you, and forever I will faithfully offer to you a tithe of all that comes to me."

Then Uncle Jacob traveled on from there, and found his way to the land of Haran, and came at last to the home of Uncle Laban. "I am Jacob," he said, "the son of your sister Rebekah, who was given in marriage to Isaac son of Abraham." As he told Uncle Laban the family history of what had happened in the decades since the wedding of Isaac and Rebekah, perhaps he shaded some of the details to make himself look a little better: it seems that he might have left out some of the details about stealing his brother's blessing, and things like that. At any rate, Uncle Laban recognized the family resemblance in the face of the traveler standing before him, and he welcomed Uncle Jacob into his home.

There were two daughters in this household, Leah and Rachel. Uncle Jacob immediately fell for the younger of the two, Rachel: a lovely and vivacious maiden. As for Leah, there was something about her eyes, although the stories differ as to exactly what that was. Some say she might have been nearsighted; others propose that perhaps her eyes did not match in color, or that she may have been quite shy and kept her eyes turned downward.

The negotiations were interesting. Uncle Laban could tell that Jacob was completely smitten with Rachel. So Uncle Laban made a great show of reluctance; he reminisced about Rachel's childhood, he told stories about her cleverness, and he rambled on about how precious she was to her mother, and about how he didn't know if he could really give her in marriage to someone who would take her far away from her family. On and on he went, and Uncle Jacob tried to listen patiently; but finally he blurted out, "So. What is the bottom line?"

And Uncle Laban carefully did not smile, as he made his first offer, an outrageous offer: seven years of service, in exchange for the bride. He knew of course that Uncle Jacob would scoff at that. No one ever accepts the first offer; it just gives the buyer and the seller a number to start with, so that negotiations can proceed. But Uncle Jacob said, "Agreed. When will the wedding be?"

So they scheduled the wedding, and everyone from all the villages round about came for the celebration: a seven-day-long celebratory feast. As the sun was setting on the first evening of that week, the torches were lit, and everyone began to sing and march in the procession. Soon the groom was holding hands with the bride, modestly hidden behind her veil, as the two stood before everyone and gave their promises: and then they retired to the bridal tent, followed by the cheers and teasing and well-wishing of all the crowd, who went on drinking and carousing until very late that night.

When Uncle Jacob awoke in the morning he rolled over and reached for his bride, and by the light of day he discovered that the woman in his bed was Leah. Ah, to have seen the look on his face at that moment! He started to jump up from the bed, planning to storm into Uncle Laban's tent and confront him with wild screams of outrage. But at the same time he felt like such a fool; he hardly knew if he could even show his face outside the tent at all.

Later that morning he stood face to face with Uncle Laban: "You tricked me! We agreed that I would serve you for seven years, in exchange for you giving me your daughter Rachel as my wife. But you have cheated me. How could you have done this, working a switch and putting a different girl in my bed?"

Uncle Laban looked surprised, and pained. The pain might have been from the harshness of Uncle Jacob's tone of voice, or it might have been the effects of the hangover from the long night of drinking. "Tricked you? But—heavens, I thought you knew. It has always been our custom that the younger daughter cannot be given in marriage before the older one. I guess it never occurred to me that you wouldn't be aware of that.

"Well," said Uncle Laban. "I don't want you to feel like you've been taken advantage of. After all, we are family now. Tell you what I'm gonna do. Complete the week's celebration with your bride, Leah—it would be a shameful thing, for her and for you and for all the family, don't you think, if you did anything else—and then I'll give you Rachel as your bride as well, in exchange for an additional seven years of service."

The stories do not tell us how Uncle Jacob felt about this adjustment to the deal. Was he glad that he would indeed get Rachel as his bride? Was he dismayed that the deal suddenly included an additional seven years of labor that would build his uncle's fortune but not his own? No one knows; if Uncle Jacob told anyone how he felt, it never became part of any of the stories that have been handed down. They simply indicate that Jacob accepted this new arrangement. In the end he had his beloved Rachel, and also her sister Leah; and his payment turned out to be fourteen years of servitude to his Uncle Laban.

Uncle Laban gave a servant girl to each of his daughters: Zilpah as servant to Leah, and Bilhah to Rachel. It would turn out that each of the daughters would eventually give her servant as concubine to Uncle Jacob, for the sake of bearing more children, to build the family. To these four women, then, were born thirteen children. Aunt Leah was the mother of the first four: Reuben, Simeon, Levi, and Judah. Aunt Rachel nearly went crazy with jealousy, as her sister Leah brought forth one child after another; and so it was that she gave her servant Bilhah to her husband Jacob to bear children in her name; and Aunt Bilhah bore Dan, and then Naphtali. Not to be outdone, Aunt Leah gave her servant Zilpah to her husband, and Aunt Zilpah bore Gad, and then Asher. Then Aunt Leah bore two more sons, Issachar and Zebulun, and then a daughter, Dinah. Then God remembered Rachel, and blessed her with a son, whom she named Joseph. And although it is getting ahead of the story a little, I will tell you that many years later Rachel bore another son, Benjamin.

These twelve sons—Reuben, Simeon, Levi, Judah, Dan, Naphtali, Gad, Asher, Issachar, Zebulun, Joseph, and Benjamin—would eventually have children and grandchildren of their own, who would comprise twelve great tribes, forming a whole nation. But that also would be in the future.

So the years passed, with Uncle Jacob and his brood living in Haran, working for Uncle Laban, and slowly building up a small flock of their own animals amidst the larger flocks of Uncle Laban. Until the time came when they left Haran and headed back home. What a crew. Traveling along, day by day. Uncle Jacob sent messengers ahead, to let his folks and Uncle Red know that after all these years he was coming home. The messengers came back with the word that Uncle Red had said "Isn't that nice." And that then Uncle Red had started gathering together a ground of armed men—400 of them in all—and began preparations to march to meet Uncle Jacob and his family.

When Uncle Jacob heard this report of his brother with a troop of soldiers on the move, it did not sound like good news. Uncle Jacob's response to this news turned out not to be his finest moment.

It was in the middle of a day's travel that the messengers returned. The family caravan was resting in the shade of the trees next to the Jabbok brook, refilling water skins and getting ready to ford the brook and travel for a few more hours before making camp for the night. "We will travel further," Uncle Jacob said, "but we will split up into groups, with some space between groups." And so it was that he set up all his family and all his goods in a new order of march. The cattle, along with most of the servants, were in the first group, up front. A mile in back of them came the second group, with Aunt Leah, along with Aunt Ziphrah and Aunt Bilhah and their children. The third group was small, just Aunt Rachel and her son, Joseph. Group by group he sent them forward, reckoning that this setup gave him his best chance of survival. When Uncle Red and his band of soldiers came across the first group, if they were bent on revenge they would kill or enslave the servants and steal all the cattle, and maybe be satisfied with that plunder—and at least the wives and children would escape. And if that did not work, they would next attack Aunt Leah and her group, and take them as slaves and concubines, and be satisfied—and at least Rachel and her son, Joseph, would escape. And if even that didn't work—if Uncle Jacob lost all his wealth and all his family to his brother's wrath—then at least he himself would have ample opportunity to hear the screams of terrified cattle and people, which would give him enough time to slink off and hide and escape.

As I say, this was not Uncle Jacob's finest moment. For while he sent each group forward in the line of march, he himself did not join the end of the line at all. He stayed on the other side of the Jabbok brook.

It took all afternoon to send everyone along, with a delay between each of the groups. The sun was low by the time Aunt Rachel and Joseph, just a lad at this point, waded across the brook and headed south; they had enough time to walk perhaps a mile or two before they would need to find a likely spot to camp, alone for the night, unprotected from beasts hunting in the dark. Uncle Jacob stood there, watching them disappear from sight. And then he stood alone, as the shadows deepened.

Then God showed up. It wasn't as if God had been absent during the three decades or so, between this event and the time when Uncle Jacob saw him in his dream at Bethel. God is present all the time: but invisibly, quietly, heard in the silence, rather than appearing in a physical or visible or bodily form.

But God actually showed up in human form this time, and ambushed Uncle Jacob. God was hiding in the tall grass, and suddenly grabbed Uncle Jacob by the heel and threw him to the ground, and then leaped forward to pin him down in the dust. I think that was sneaky of God, running the "at your heels" strategy on Uncle Jacob. God can be sly like that, sometimes. But even though Uncle Jacob was caught off guard by this ambush, he was still slick as a weasel, and he squirmed out of the pin and wrestled his way around into a clinch.

All night they wrestled, hot and sweaty. You would think that God would just blink, God would just *decide*, and Uncle Jacob would be bounced across the ground a few times and crash into a tree and would find himself dazed and staring up at the stars; but God was apparently playing fair at this point, wrestling man to man, as it were. And Uncle Jacob managed to do surprisingly well, wrestling with God and not getting thrown, not giving up. Finally God was willing to call it a draw, and said, "All right, that's enough. Time to stop."

But Uncle Jacob would not quit, even then. So God touched him on the hip, and put his hip out of joint—bam, just like that. And still Uncle Jacob hung on: agony twisting his nerves, he still would not let go. "Really, that's enough," said God. "You've done well, and I'm proud of you. But just let go now."

And Uncle Jacob said, "I won't let go unless you bless me."

Then God smiled and said, "Tell me your name." I always find it fascinating when God asks for information like that. I guess you kind of figure that being omniscient and all, God can't need the information. Like when God puts you to the test in some way, and you think, "Was this necessary? Maybe I myself didn't know for sure how I would respond, in the midst of this crisis you gave me, but aren't you already supposed to know these things, before they ever happen?"

"Tell me your name," said God, and Uncle Jacob replied, "I am Jacob." All the anguish and ambiguity of his name hung there in the air of that early dawn. I am "At-Your-Heels." All my life I have been wearing this name, a name that could tell you that "I've got your back," or it could tell you "I will ambush you." And my whole life has lived up to the ambiguity of this name: I've always wanted to be the steadfast friend, but mostly I seem to end up being the sly ambusher.

And then God said this: "I give you a new name: you are Israel."

Ha! That's the name God gave him, and this new name 'Israel' also has an ambiguous meaning. It means "he strives with God." But does that mean he strives *against* God, or he strives *on the side of* God? *He strives with God* because he opposes God's purpose, because he likes his own ideas better? Or *He strives with God* because God's purpose often encounters resistance from the human race, and therefore is not something that always happens automatically; instead, it often turns out to be a challenge and a struggle to bring God's purpose to fruition, but Uncle Jacob's new name would be *he strives with God* because he is on God's side in the struggle to establish God's good purpose, and Uncle Jacob will put all his energy into seeing God's purpose come true?

Down the generations, as the children of Israel, as the descendants within this great extended family, this story tells us who we are. We are those who strive with God, and this same ambiguity applies to us, doesn't it? So many times we have been striving against God, disobeying or ignoring the word that our Lord has given us. And yet, and yet: despite all those times, we are the people who give our loyalty to God; we are the people who strive with God, striving to fulfill the purposes of the kingdom of heaven. We strive with God: in confusion, in rebellion, and yet finally in repentance and restoration and renewed loyalty.

4

Moriah

PEOPLE SHOULD KNOW BETTER than to disregard an old woman, but they do it all the time. They figure they can get away with it, because old women usually don't have much physical strength to fight back, or much influence in clan politics, and the bloom of their youthful beauty has pretty well faded.

I should know. They have thought they could discount me so many times. It's so easy to read what they are thinking: never mind about her, she doesn't matter, no need to consult with her about the plans. We'll just make the decisions, and she'll have to go along in the end.

But we old women still have power: enough power that they fear us. We can no longer turn men's heads just by walking past or offering a shy smile. We have so little public voice, to offer an argument to steer the actions of the clan. What reason, then, for anyone to fear us?

But they do fear us. They fear our power.

They fear us when we are nubile virgins, and the power of our beauty can make them forget all their other plans and think of only one thing. They fear us when we are young brides and when we are mothers; our husbands fear that the arousal they feel toward other men's wives will be felt by other men toward their own wife. They fear us because of their own feelings. Of course, they could respond with self-discipline instead of with fear. They could insist that men must grow up and accept the responsibility for their attitudes and actions; they could insist that a man must learn to be man enough to control his own behavior, man enough to hold the rein on his own lust. But instead they fear us and blame us and seek to hide us away.

And even though they would wish to disregard us, often they fear us still when we become grandmothers, and the power of our family leadership gives us standing among the young girls and the expectant mothers and the new mothers. Many a young husband has assumed he could simply make a decision about what should happen, could stubbornly insist on some foolishness he has dreamed up and his wife and children will of necessity follow his mandate: and then, fortunately for him, his folly has been thwarted by the wisdom of a grandmother. Such young men could learn to be grateful for the times that grandmothers have saved them from their bad decisions; but instead they fear us.

They fear us when we have become aged, and the power of our memory reaches deep into family lore and declares stories with more depth and nuance than they wish to hear. So often the young wish for simple solutions: the answers is this, it is not that. But the old women know the lore, the depth of nearly-forgotten stories that need to be spoken: for these stories tell us once again who we are, in the complexity and mystery of how God called our family into existence.

I have been a young bride, and have watched how the eyes of my husband—and other men as well—are drawn to the curve of a breast, or the hint of a smile, or even the movement of a woman's wrist while she kneads dough for the day's bread. Men are so easily aroused, and they succumb so quickly!

I have been a grandmother. I have watched how the eyes of my husband were drawn to the curves of younger women; and I learned how to keep him well satisfied and happy with his own wife in his own bed. And I learned how to be a family leader with the young brides and new mothers.

And now I am an old woman, with nearly 90 summers gone by. My husband is dead and my sons are dead, and two of my daughters have died as well, but my grandchildren and great-grandchildren are many, and they thrive within the clan. And I bring the power of memory, as I tell a story of our family, the story of another old woman: Aunt Sarai.

You all remember, I am sure, the stories of the wedding of Uncle Avram and Aunt Sarai. What a feast that was! She was such a lovely bride. In the weeks and months that followed everyone remarked on how radiantly happy the two of them were with each other. But the first year of their marriage came to an end with no pregnancy. The second year, the third year, the same.

Then it came to pass that they left their home and journeyed into the wilderness, following the prompting of God, not knowing where

God might take them. And here is the first thing that you must note: in the early years at home, and in the years of journeying through the wilderness, Uncle Avram did not take another woman to his bed, in order to breed sons. Men are so easily aroused, and they succumb so quickly; and a man of Uncle Avram's means would be an attractive match for many a pretty girl; but he did not take another woman.

It was because Sarai loved her Avram with a fierce love, with a passion that was strong from year to year. It doesn't always happen that way, as I am sure you know. Sometimes with the passing of years husbands and wives learn to tolerate each other, or to ignore each other, and their encounters of love become rare and brief and empty. Not so with Aunt Sarai and Uncle Avram. Into their middle years and into their old age they continued to find delight and comfort and joy in each other's love.

But the ache of childlessness remained in their hearts. Perhaps it was like the soreness in an old woman's shoulder that never become completely crippling yet never seems to get better. On the outside they seemed happy enough, but the longing for a child never completely faded away. God had made a promise to them, a promise that from their offspring a mighty nation would arise, and a blessing would come to all the world from their descendants. But didn't a nation full of descendants have to start with a single baby? How could any of this promise ever come true, if they never had a child?

Aunt Sarai decided to give her slave girl, Hagar, to her husband Avram. All these decades Avram had slept only with her; now he would sleep with this young Egyptian girl, and perhaps in this way a baby would be born that would fulfill God's promise. It was a scary choice for Aunt Sarai, as it would be for any woman: giving her husband to find pleasure in a younger woman's body.

It did not turn out well. Hagar did indeed become pregnant, as everyone had hoped. But when it happened, Hagar exulted. She would bear a child, and even though she herself was a slave, her child would not be: her child would inherit all the wealth of her master.

Aunt Sarai did not handle this well. The relationship between her and her slave girl was never the same. And after Aunt Sarai had had a child of her own, a miracle baby born more than a decade later, she drove Hagar and her son Ishmael out of the camp, to die in the wilderness. It was clear that her own son, Isaac, was the child of the promise.

Hagar and Ishmael could just go die. They did not die, as it turns out; but not because Aunt Sarai gave any thought at all to keeping them alive.

Then came the day, when the boy had grown to be a sturdy and energetic lad, when God said to Uncle Avram, "Take your son, your only son, Isaac, whom you love, and go with him to the land of Moriah, and sacrifice him on the mountain there as a sacrifice to me."

It is one of the most fearsome stories we ever tell. But most people, when they tell it, assume that Aunt Sarai did not know that God had said this to Uncle Avram. Perhaps they assume that Uncle Avram did not tell her what the voice of God had said to him, because he feared her power: people sometimes assume Uncle Avram was ready to obey this command, but might have been afraid that Aunt Sarai would find the way to contradict the word of the Lord. Or perhaps people assume that Uncle Avram was afraid of the contradiction in his own soul, the contradiction between his love for his son and his love for his God: people sometimes assume the balance in his heart was teetering between obeying the Lord's command and refusing to do so, and they assume that Uncle Avram might have feared that if he gave Aunt Sarai a chance to speak, she might tip the balance the wrong way.

Sometimes people just shrug and say that the way they heard it, the story just never says whether Aunt Sarai knew or not. And so without even realizing it, they make the assumption that there is nothing to say about Aunt Sarai here; and they leave her out.

Thus, one way or the other, people assume that Aunt Sarai had no part in the story of Uncle Avram and Uncle Isaac. It is one of the fiercest stories in our family history—"go, and sacrifice your son as a burnt offering to me!"—and people assume that this story only had to do with Uncle Avram and Uncle Isaac. When people tell this story they either assume that Uncle Avram deliberately left Aunt Sarai out, or else they suppose that because they have no information it is right to leave Aunt Sarai out.

One of the advantages of being an old woman is that I see this story from an old woman's perspective. I can see how their marriage must have weathered one crisis after another: the crisis of Aunt Sarai never becoming pregnant, the crisis of leaving home, the crisis with Pharoah's household in Egypt, the crisis with Lot and his family, the crisis of Hagar and Ishmael, the crisis when God came to dinner and Sarai laughed at the wonder and absurdity of it all. And how did they weather all these crises? By never discussing any of them, never working them through in extensive conversation? Hardly. It was rather through many conversations, talking early in the day, talking over the noonday and evening meals, pillow talk at night, talking of the worries and the hopes and the challenges and the details that make up a couple's life.

And so to me it seems most likely that Aunt Sarai knew what God had said: that she knew that God had said, "Take your son, your only son, Isaac, whom you love." God spoke these words to Uncle Avram, and yet they address most clearly the heart of Aunt Sarai: for of the two of them, she was the spouse for whom it was true that she had only one son, whom she loved. Uncle Avram had two sons, and he loved them both. But Aunt Sarai did not claim two sons: she only claimed one, and she loved that one son and not the other.

When the command came to Uncle Avram, he would need to make preparations to travel for several days, to the land of Moriah. Cutting dried wood for the sacrifice. Assembling food in sacks for the journey. In a nomadic family, the family ordinarily travels together: if part of the family goes, all the family goes. Fold the tents, drive the herds to new pastureland. So to presume that Uncle Avram made these preparations and Aunt Sarai never asked, "What are you doing?"—that is quite a presumption.

What would it be like for Uncle Avram, when God spoke to him and filled his heart with trembling at this awful thing God commanded him to do? It would be strange if we imagined that Aunt Sarai did not notice this. It would be strange to suppose that in the quiet moments in the evening Aunt Sarai would never have asked what it was that made Uncle Avram so noticeably anxious. And when she asked, it is easy enough to see that he would have been afraid to tell her—and also afraid not to tell her. And that they would have ended up having a fierce and teary conversation, long into the dark.

So then, if you will listen to the wisdom and experience of an old old woman, I can tell you how I think the story must have gone.

God spoke to Avram, and his heart trembled. And at supper that night, Aunt Sarai noticed that he was quiet and troubled, and she asked how he was feeling.

Uncle Avram replied that he was fine, yet it was clear that his thoughts were actually quite distant. And Aunt Sarai said to herself, "No, he is not fine. I wonder what it is that is troubling him."

That evening, with the stars shining bright, she sat next to him and held his hand, as they so often did. He did not speak. She felt the tremble in his hand. "Is it frailty or old age?" she asked herself. "We have enjoyed good health for so many years, but we are far past middle age now." And then she spoke up. "You are so quiet this evening. Is there some concern?"

Uncle Avram did not speak for the longest time. She asked again, and this time he said, "No, nothing." And as he said it, he knew that it was wrong, that it was a lie. In all the crises of his life there had never been a bigger concern. Yet he had to keep silent; how could he speak such a thing? And as he was reckoning with this dishonesty, Aunt Sarai could read the hesitation and the despair in Uncle Avram's soul clearly enough to know that it must be some very serious matter indeed.

"Well, it is late," she said. She said it with the hint of a suggestion in her voice. "I am going to bed." Husbands and wives learn to speak in small nuances; this was one of the nuances that they had learned, in their long decades together. It would always bring a quirky little grin to the corner of Uncle Avram's mouth, as he recognized the invitation in that tone of voice. But on this occasion he did not smile. He simply said, "You go on. I'll be there in a little while."

So Aunt Sarai went inside and got ready for bed. Uncle Avram had said he would be there in a little while, but he waited much longer than that. He waited until he was sure she would be asleep, and then he crept into the tent and slid into bed as silently as moonlight, so that he would not awaken her.

But she was still awake, and her arms and legs wrapped around him in fierce embrace, her hands gripping his shoulders and, despite his momentary resistance, drawing him out of his silent despair and into her love. And in the end he was weeping great tears as she cradled his head on her breasts, and she wept too, as all the story came tumbling out.

And Aunt Sarai heard the echo of the words God had spoken to her Avram: the command to sacrifice "your son, your only son Isaac, whom you love." She thought of the two sons, Ishmael and Isaac, and thought that she would gladly sacrifice Ishmael. She had been quite willing to sacrifice Ishmael and Hagar both, in order to ensure the inheritance of her son, her only son, the one whom she loved. It had been wrong. She had been wrong. She knew that, now. Truly she had known it then as well, but her anger and jealousy and pride had been strong, and she had insisted that Hagar and Ishmael be sent out to the wilderness, to die there.

She still held the face of her now-sleeping husband against her skin, unable to sleep with his weight pressing uncomfortably on her. Yet Aunt Sarai did not slide away to the far side of the bed. She held on to him, and allowed her soul to cry out to God.

"Why are you asking this of us?" she asked. "This is the son you promised us. All your promises of blessings for all the generations are to be established in this child. How then can you claim him as a sacrifice?"

God did not reply.

It is difficult to scream at God when your husband is sleeping on your chest and you don't want to wake him: it is difficult at such a moment to pour out all your anger, to rage at the unfairness and the stupidity of God's actions. Such actions might well be inconsequential details to the God of the universe, yet they are life-and-death decisions, flooding your soul with such grief and despair that you want to shriek in agony, and it is hard to do that in silence. Yet that's what Aunt Sarai did, with tears and sobs and rage, all without making a single sound.

In her soul Aunt Sarai railed, pouring out her silent accusations toward God with a vehemence few have matched in all the long generations—even when others have had the advantage of making noise. "No! No! No! You must not do this, O God of righteousness: it is wrong wrong wrong!" She was not afraid to let such strong accusations against the Almighty fill her heart, sensing that the Almighty would be strong enough to handle the rage in her soul. And if not, if God struck her dead for her opposition, she would be no worse off.

God did not strike her dead. God made no reply at all.

Aunt Sarai tried bargaining: "If there needs to be a human sacrifice, then I will do it," she prayed. "I was wrong about Hagar and Ishmael, but I am not wrong about this. If you need for someone to die, then you may kill me. But change your mind and spare my son, my only son Isaac, whom I love more than my own life."

And again, God did not respond.

Aunt Sarai pointed out the injustice of this. In the ordinary course of events, she should have had, by her age, more great-grandchildren and great-great-grandchildren than she could easily keep track of, but instead she had only this one boy, still just a lad. She knew she could not wish such a disaster on anybody else; she had come to know that from having wished disaster on Hagar. Yet if God needed the sacrifice of a child, why not ask it from some family with twenty grandsons? Why was God picking on her? Surely if some woman had twenty grandsons and lost one, it would be a tragedy, but she would still have a family filled with descendants. But Aunt Sarai only had one child, and the overwhelming cruelty of God in deliberately commanding them to sacrifice the life of their beloved son—this was more than a human soul could bear.

And still God did not reply.

"I won't allow it," she said to herself. "And that is that. We will run away. I'll tell Avram, and he will agree and we will move our tents and our possessions far away. If Avram won't agree, then I will take the boy myself and we will run away into the wilderness, just the two of us, and leave behind Avram and his God. Maybe we will die in the desert, but it's better than just quietly acquiescing to this outrageous demand from God."

And God was still silent—and yet somehow this silence was different. In this silence she sensed that God was there. Her heart beat fast as she realized that there was something—an invitation?—yes, an invitation from God to consider what she had just decided.

So Aunt Sarai considered.

It is a choice between my son and my God, she realized. I love many things in this life: crisp mornings, and tender roast lamb with garlic and lentils, and cool water and bright flowers. I love my husband Avram in a hundred ways, and I will till the day I die. And I love you, O Lord my God, for all the mystery and majesty of who you are, no matter how much I fail to understand what you want or why. But O God, I love my son. I love my son best of all.

As Aunt Sarai considered all this, she saw it, and she spoke it, in the quiet of her soul: That's what this is all about, isn't it? As God you demand first place in our loyalty. We may not let anything else have our most absolute devotion.

And you are forcing me to make this choice. You have set this up so that I would see this choice in the starkest way possible: to whom will the utter depths of my soul's devotion be given?

The tears flowed unheeded. "O God, don't make me choose, I beg you." She felt her arms trembling; they were still wrapped around her sleeping husband's shoulder and head, and she tried to calm the trembling but she could not. "Don't make me choose. Let me love you, and love my son, and don't put me to this test, to decide which I love the most. Please."

For long aching moments the silence within the silence simply grew deeper. God did not speak, and Aunt Sarai could not. It was all she could do to breathe, and maybe she would not even be able to do that. Somehow she found the courage to pray on. "Can I not simply say that I love you best of all? I do not understand how you will fulfill your promise to establish many generations of inheritance through this son, if this son lies dead on a sacrificial altar. Perhaps I do not need to understand that. Perhaps I do not need to understand anything other than the fact that you have it in your control. Perhaps I do not need anything but you. All right. I see that. I must not claim anything for myself but you. I must not claim that my husband is mine and therefore not yours. I must not claim that my own breath, my own life, is mine and not yours."

Aunt Sarai paused there. She knew what she needed to say next. She took a very large breath, almost as if it would be her very last breath, and then she spoke again in the silence of her soul: "I must not claim that my son is mine and not yours." She felt the shift as the world changed in that moment: expressing those words had made something different. Reality had been one way; now reality was another way. Just like any idol worshiper, bowing down before a brazen image of Astarte, offering devotion before a statue of Baal, she saw that her heart had idolized her son Isaac, and had set him in the place of first importance and loyalty. Her idolatry had been more subtle than others, perhaps, but nonetheless real. She saw it. "It was true, my God. But it is true no more. I worship you alone."

And then, greatly daring: "May it be, O Lord my God, that you look on the truth in my heart, and see that in all things, even in this, I bow before you: and thus might you grant to my son his life, that he may live as your servant."

And God made no reply. In the utter clarity of that moment Aunt Sarai knew that there was nothing else she could say, and the anguish of her soul emerged in a great wail of mourning, and her whole body was wracked with sobs.

It awakened Uncle Avram, of course. He did not know what it was at first, and so he did what any sensible man would do, in such a moment: he rolled onto his back, pulled her onto his chest, wrapped her in his arms, and held her while she wept, there in the early dawn. The ache in his own soul reminded him why she wept, and he felt his own tears flowing on his cheekbones and earlobes. He wanted to wipe them away, but he kept his arms wrapped around his wife and let the tears flow unchecked.

Aunt Sarai sobbed for a long time, great ragged breaths, and Uncle Avram held her and kissed the top of her head. He wanted to say something comforting, like "It will be all right," but he knew that that was a lie, it was not going to be all right, it was devastating and it would keep on being devastating. All he could do was hold her, and wait. Finally she quieted. Aunt Sarai became so still he could just feel the movements of her breathing; and Uncle Avram thought she had fallen asleep.

But she had not, as he discovered in a moment as she began to make love with astonishing intensity. Avram had long known how fortunate a man he was, to have a wife who desired his love so well; and she had surprised him with lovemaking many times. Yet he thought she had never expressed such desperation before. And somehow he knew this moment was not about desire or pleasure. It was not about comfort or closeness. It was about life, in the face of death.

When their breathing calmed once again, Uncle Avram thought, "Now she will sleep." But again, she did not. She got out of bed, pulled on her clothing, and went out to put together the supplies that Avram would need for the journey to Moriah.

So Uncle Avram got dressed, and went out in the early morning light. There was a dead tree lying on the ground at the edge of the encampment; he had dragged it there with a couple of oxen, a few days earlier, and now he took his axe and began to cut a load of firewood from it, to use for the burnt offering. The servants were up and around as well, and Uncle Avram instructed a couple of them to get ready for several days of travel. The servants took the wood and loaded it onto one of the donkeys. Aunt Sarai brought out the bag of supplies she had put together, and the servants loaded that as well. Isaac had been awakened by the sound of the axe, and even though he was still half asleep he could tell that something unusual was going on. He sat in the doorway of his tent and put on his sandals.

One of the servants had prepared a fire jar as well. This was a medium-sized clay bucket, with a lengthy strap of thick leather for a handle. This bucket would be filled with burning coals from the fire, and the leather strap would then be wrapped around the end of a wooden staff. You'd burn your hand, if you tried to carry a bucket of live coals by the handle; but if you used a wooden staff, supported over your shoulder, you could carry a fire jar without burning your hand.

Aunt Sarai watched them as they walked away. She had hugged Isaac for a moment before he had wriggled away with a boy's awkwardness at being embraced by his mother. She wanted to hold onto him for much longer, long enough to remember this one last hug for the rest of her life: but she did not hang on when he squirmed, she let him go, not trusting herself to keep from crying if she held on any longer. Aunt Sarai watched them, as they headed toward the curve in the road, Avram and Isaac walking together in front, Isaac chattering away, and the two servants following, one leading the laden donkey, the other carrying the oak staff across his shoulder, with the fire jar out at the end.

Aunt Sarai watched them as they rounded the curve and were lost to sight, and she felt the pang of loss and grief and loneliness that women have always felt when their husbands and sons have gone off to face death, knowing that a terrible cost is being paid, knowing that their lives are being changed, against their will, and knowing there is nothing they can do to affect the outcome. Aunt Sarai stood there, staring down the empty road as if she could still see them, as if she could still see her son, her only son Isaac, whom she loved, for a moment longer.

Later she would find out what had happened. She would find out that they had traveled and camped out for two days, keeping the fire alive in the jar by dropping pieces of wood in several times a day, and using those hot coals to start their fire each evening to cook their meal. Each night they banked the fire to burn through the night, and each morning they built the fire up again to make fresh coals, and reloaded them into the fire jar before they continued on their way.

Mid-morning on the third day Avram had seen the mountain, and known that this was the appointed place. He told the two servants to unload the donkey and wait where they were. They loaded the bundle of sacrificial firewood onto Isaac's back. Over his left shoulder Avram supported the oak staff from which the fire jar hung, and in his right hand he carried the slaughtering knife.

It was only when Uncle Avram told her afterwards what had happened that Aunt Sarai learned of Isaac's curious question: we have the wood and the fire, but we don't have a lamb for the burnt offering. Avram had answered, "God will provide." Avram had hated himself at that moment. The words had come to his lips and had answered his son's question, and the words expressed the longing of his heart, but Uncle Avram could not see any way that God could provide a way out of this horrible demand.

And so Uncle Avram, an old man and feeling older with every step he took, and Uncle Isaac, still a lad of ten, came to the top of the mountain. They set their items on the ground, and began selecting stones: large stones, small boulders, really, which Uncle Avram rolled into place and then fitted them together, building them into an altar. He laid the wood in order across the top of the altar, tinder and kindling and branches, set to blaze up fast and burn hot for a short while, just long enough to consume the offering.

Then Uncle Avram took his son, and bound his hands and feet, and lifted him up and placed him on top of the wood. "What are you doing?" Isaac had screamed in panic.

Avram looked at his son. He had to answer him. Surely the boy deserved an answer. But what answer was there? Finally he said, "This is what God demands."

"But why? Why does God demand that I be killed?"

There was no answer to that: or at least, no answer that Avram knew. He just shook his head.

"Wait! What about 'God will provide' ?"

There was no answer to that, either. Avram took the knife, determined to move quickly, for he knew that if he delayed further he would lose his nerve entirely. When Aunt Sarai heard it, she knew she would already have lost her nerve, if she had been there. Avram told her that he feared that this sight was burned into his eyes forever: the harsh sunshine lighting every detail of the altar and the wood and Isaac's trembling body, twisting against the ropes, and the desperate tears on his face as he looked at the knife being raised in his father's hand.

It was in that moment that God stayed Avram's hand. The angel of the Lord called out his name: and Uncle Avram had replied, "Here I am."

The angel said, "Do not harm the boy in any way, for now I know that your heart truly reveres God, since you have not withheld your son, your only son, from me."

So Uncle Avram cut the ropes and set his son free. And a movement caught his eye. He saw a ram, caught in a thicket by its horns. It was a short distance away, and perhaps not immediately visible from every angle; yet Uncle Avram felt sure that they would have seen that ram earlier, if it had been there during the time when they were looking around in every direction to select and gather the stones for the altar. And so Uncle Avram knew that this ram had been set there by the Lord. "The Lord will provide" indeed, he thought. And he walked to the ram, dragged it to the altar and killed it, and laid this offering, provided by God, on top of the wood. Uncle Avram held the oak staff with the clay jar filled with hot coals over the tinder and kindling that he had arranged at the end of the altar, and nodded to Isaac his son: and Isaac took a stick and turned the jar over, so that the burning coals fell into the tinder, setting it ablaze. Father and son stood there together, watching the flame spread along the altar and engulf the dead goat.

"That could be me," thought young Uncle Isaac. "I do not know why God wanted to kill me. I do not know why God repented. But indeed, the Lord has provided, and I am still alive."

"That could be my son," thought Uncle Avram. "I still do not know why you wanted to kill him, O God. I do not know why you changed your mind. You said, 'Now I know that your heart truly reveres God, Avram'—but why did you need to do this in order to know? *Now* you know? Don't you always know the thoughts and intentions of our hearts? Why do you need to set up such a severe test in order to find out?"

To the end of his days, that was a puzzle to Uncle Avram.

But when he recounted to Aunt Sarai all that had happened, she understood.

Aunt Sarai was waiting, when they came home, so full of dread. She knew that it would rip her heart out when she saw Avram and the servants returning without Isaac. It was ripping her heart out already, inch by anguished inch, to wait and wait, helplessly left behind. When she looked down the road she saw them coming: four of them. Four? Four! She ran down the road to meet them, weeping in astonishment and joy when Isaac came running up to her, with a fierce embrace. Isaac had always been so full of chatter, but now he was feeling the flood of astonishing emotions that he could not put into words, and so they simply held on to each other in silence..

In the days that followed Isaac did not speak of what he had experienced. He did not speak of it, for many years: and when he did finally pass this story along, he never said much. Probably Aunt Sarai his mother understood it as well as anyone, just from that silent tearful hug in those moments as she felt his trembling slowly ebb.

Uncle Avram did share what had happened, how God had stayed his hand and then had said "Now I know." He shared how puzzling that had been, how he didn't understand why God had needed such an event in order to know.

Aunt Sarai listened, and nodded. Uncle Avram thought she was nodding in sympathy with how it was hard to understand why God needed such a test in order to know. She knew he was thinking that, and she did not tell him otherwise.

But in truth she was nodding because she actually did understand. She understood that something had happened, through this heart-rending test, something had happened that had made the world different. God doesn't know everything, she thought: God knows only those things that are true. God doesn't know anything that is false. God doesn't know anything that is maybe. God only knows the things that are true.

Aunt Sarai saw what it meant: the reason that God hadn't known before, the reason God only knew it "now," was that her devotion to God, even beyond her love for herself, her husband, and her son, was only finally true when her Avram had indeed carried her surrender, and his own as well, all the way to that terrible moment.

That's the kind of hard-won insight an old woman like Aunt Sarai could have. Of course, the story is different, from Aunt Hagar's perspective. You'd never expect to hear much from her—an Egyptian slave girl. And yet she had such interesting conversations with God. You need to hear her story, too.

5

Get Out!

GOD SPOKE TO UNCLE Abram, and told him he had to leave his homeland and family. "Get out of this country where you live now, this place of your extended family and your birth," said God, "and go to the place I will show you. For I am going to make you a great nation; I will bless you, and guard you. And indeed, I have a plan to bless all the nations of the earth through you."

Uncle Abram found it quite surprising as he recognized that God was addressing him. It was quite an amazing thing, to consider that God had a plan to bless Abram and his family. It was even more astonishing to suppose that God had a plan to bless all the nations of the earth through him. Yet perhaps the part that felt most shocking to Uncle Abram was the command to get out of his native land. Leave behind his cousins and all the intricate web of family interdependence? It was nearly unthinkable. If it had not been God who had spoken, it would indeed be unthinkable. Yet when the Almighty tells you to get out, it makes you give serious consideration to possibilities you would never have dreamed of before.

So it came to pass that Uncle Abram got out. He took Sarai his wife, and his nephew Lot with his wife and two little girls, and his cattle and his servants and his tents. They made their way west, one day's journey at a time, and camped night by night in places with grass and water, when they could. Often they could not, and spent the night listening to the anxious lowing of the tired and hungry and thirsty cattle.

Year by year they traveled, sometimes at a different campsite every night for weeks on end, sometimes staying in one spot for several months. Everyone got very good at setting up camp in the evening, and breaking camp and loading everything onto the animals in the morning.

They never knew for sure how long they would stay anywhere. Uncle Abram would wake up in the early dawn, look around in the half-light, and go about his morning routine—or he would simply say, "All right, let's move." And when he said that, everything would be loaded and they would be on their way in less than an hour.

They had traveled from one place to another: up to the north, one time, nearly to Damascus; along the coast, in what would become the land of the Philistines; and one time they journeyed all the way south to Egypt, in order to do business there.

That trip to Egypt had made Uncle Abram quite nervous. Egypt was . . . different.

You see, when Uncle Abram and his crew were traveling, they would frequently encounter other wandering tribes, and they would visit in various small villages along the way. These meetings were always an occasion for sizing one another up. The chieftain of the other nomadic tribe or of the village would assess the risks: the risk of attacking Uncle Abram, or of being attacked by him. Uncle Abram always had dozens of young men working for him, sometimes hundreds, and so he did not look like an easy target to other groups. He always told those whom he met that he came in peace. But that's what any raider would say, if he was planning a sneak attack on you: so just because Uncle Abram said he came in peace, that didn't make everyone feel peaceful. Uncle Abram wanted to be a man of peace, and generally so did the people of the villages and tribes he encountered. Even so, whenever they were camped close enough, within nighttime raiding distance, no one got much sleep on either side. Still, most of the time nobody actually attacked.

But Egypt: Egypt was different. When Uncle Abram thought about Egypt, he felt so anxious, because Egypt was huge. Egypt could smack him like any stray bug. Uncle Abram could defend himself against any ordinary band of raiders, whether nomads or villagers. Yet he knew he could not stand against any portion of the Egyptian army, if it ever came to a battle.

So he was determined that it must not come to a battle. He hoped to trade, to gain new animals for his flocks and herds, and new goods for his family, and perhaps some items he could sell elsewhere at a profit: but if the Egyptians decided to rob him of all his goods, Uncle Abram was prepared to let it all go. He hoped to gain wives for some of his young men, and to find husbands for some of the daughters of his servants: but if the Egyptians decided simply to seize the people of his household, Uncle Abram was prepared to let them all go. He hoped that he and Sarai would feel the blessing of God on their marriage with ongoing joy and satisfaction and goodness: but if the Egyptians decided they wanted her, Uncle Abram was prepared to let her go, too.

It must not come to a battle, thought Uncle Abram. As he considered what he must do to make sure it did not, he came to the conclusion that he should say that Sarai was not his wife, but his sister. That way, if the Egyptians decided they wanted her, they would negotiate; if they thought she was his wife, they would simply kill him and then claim the widow for themselves.

Aunt Sarai was quite astonished when Uncle Abram instructed her that if anyone asked, she was to identify herself as his sister rather than his wife. They did ask, of course, and Aunt Sarai dutifully identified herself as Uncle Abram's sister. Soon the report got back to the court of the Pharoah himself: a nomad named Abram had come to trade, he had a fairly extensive retinue, and he had with him his sister, a woman of striking beauty. The Pharoah had not been paying much attention to the long boring report his advisor had been presenting about trading with nomadic tribes present in Egypt; but when he heard about the sister of striking beauty, he perked right up. "All right," he said. "Work it out with this nomad. Make sure his traders don't get double-assessed by the customs officers. And arrange for this sister to get brought into my harem."

So it was done. Officials from the Pharoah's court came to see Uncle Abram. Uncle Abram ended up with a very favorable trade agreement, and his herds grew large as he traded with the Egyptians. He had herds of sheep and oxen, donkeys and camels, and he had families of male and female slaves to care for all these herds. And the Pharoah ended up with Aunt Sarai in his harem.

As it turns out, however, God did not like this arrangement. The story might be different, if Uncle Abram had consulted with God before he decided that he was prepared to let Aunt Sarai go to the Egyptians; but he had not done that. He had simply assumed that whatever was the price of survival, that was a price he would pay.

Yet God had a plan in mind, a plan to bless all the world through the descendants of Uncle Abram and Aunt Sarai, and this plan would not work if Uncle Abram and his great flocks and herds made their nomadic way back north out of Egypt while Aunt Sarai stayed behind in the Pharoah's harem. And so God began to afflict the Pharoah and his house with rashes and fevers and achy joints and stomach disorders. Everyone was sick and miserable. Everyone except for Aunt Sarai, that is. She was beautiful, as she made her way from room to room in the Pharoah's palace, bringing cold cloths to cool the brow of those who were feverish, and chicken soup to keep up the strength of those who were run down.

The Pharoah, feeling wretched and weak, called in his diviners to find out why all his household had become so sick. These diviners noticed, first of all, that one woman in the harem was not sick; and they found out that she was a recent addition, purchased from the family of some nomadic trader. They drew two preliminary conclusions from this. First, the woman clearly had been protected from the illness that had affected everyone else; and second, this affliction must be because of her. The most likely cause was that one of the gods must be angry with the Pharoah for bringing this woman into his harem; and that obviously meant that there was something wrong if Aunt Sarai was sleeping with the Pharoah. Yet there would not have been anything wrong with that, if the woman had been a virgin or a widow. Thus, they deduced, it must be the case that she was already some other man's wife: that must be the wrongness that had caused one of the gods to afflict the household of the Pharoah.

Yet it would hardly be worthy of the notice of any of the gods, if she were merely the wife of some slave. In order for it to matter to any of the gods, it would have to be the case that she was the wife of someone important. And that means, they concluded, that she must be the wife of the tribal chieftain himself, Uncle Abram. The man had lied, probably out of fear—they understood about lying when you are afraid—and had passed his wife off as his sister. Yet whatever god had this man under his protection was angry at the Pharoah for taking the woman into his harem. That's what the diviners reported to their master, the Pharoah, Lord of Egypt.

When the Pharoah heard that, he wanted to kill Uncle Abram and take all his goods: that's how angry he was about this. But he still felt wretched, from the illness that had drained all his strength, and he was afraid to do anything further to anger whatever god had decided to protect this nomad. So he ordered that Aunt Sarai be removed from the harem and escorted safely back to her husband, along with a message that laid the blame squarely on Uncle Abram. "You lied to me. I don't know why your god is punishing me for it, rather than you, because it is your fault that your wife ended up in my harem. You are the one who said, 'She is my sister.' Now: get out. Take your people and your animals, and get out of my land, and do not come back again." The Pharoah's officers escorted Uncle Abram and his clan out to the border, and sent them on their way.

No other details have come to us about Aunt Sarai's time in the Pharoah's court. Was it pleasant there, or awkward? Did she make friends with other women there despite the language barrier, or did she just feel like an outsider who would never be accepted by the others? And did she end up sleeping with the Pharoah? No one in the family ever handed down any stories about these things.

Although she may have been in the harem for several weeks, it's quite possible that she was never called to the Pharoah's bed. A king of a mighty nation like Egypt could easily have so many women in his harem that he could not know all their names, let alone know all their bodies in a given amount of time. Uncle Solomon, for example, many generations later: when he was king, he was famous for having three hundred wives and seven hundred concubines: a harem of a thousand women! It's hard to suppose that every single one of them got called to Uncle Solomon's bed as often as once per year.

As far as we know, Aunt Sarai never told anyone whether she had sex with the Pharoah. Uncle Abram might well have had the wisdom to know that he should not ask. It is even possible that Aunt Sarai was secretly hoping all along that that's what would happen, when Uncle Abram told her to say she was his sister: she would end up having sex with the Pharoah, and would become pregnant, and would bear a son, and then would somehow escape from the harem with her son and rejoin Uncle Abram and move back out of Egypt, and they would become a family of three. It is possible that this was part of the reason she acquiesced without offering alternatives, when Uncle Abram directed her to identify herself only as his sister and not as his wife; it is possible that this is why she accepted being sold into Pharoah's harem: not simply for fear that this was the only possibility of avoiding her husband's death, but also in the hope that she might end up with a child.

That might well be what she was thinking; but none of the family stories tell us so for sure.

Yet it is at least true that her heart was full of longing for a child. Her love for her husband ran very deep, and yet throughout their long life together there were days of deep sadness as she discovered, once again, that another month had gone by and she still was not pregnant.

She wanted a child. God had promised a child, a lineage, a heritage; indeed, God had promised that a whole nation would come, and a blessing for the whole world would come from that nation. Like the sands of the sea, like the stars in the sky, that's what the size of your family is going to be like: that's what God had promised. But if you are going to have a family of millions, down the generations, you have to have generations. If you have a husband and wife, that's one generation: but only one. If you are going to have a family of millions, you have to have a next generation. Yet month after month, there was no next generation.

Aunt Sarai wanted a child. Everyone else seemed to get pregnant, babies were born, children grew. But never Aunt Sarai. She did not want to get depressed over it. She still had a husband and servants; she was the mistress of a wealthy household, with goods and cattle and luxuries. She was in good health, really it was remarkable health for a woman her age. Many people in the world went hungry: and yet Aunt Sarai and her household had plenty of grain, healthy flocks and herds, and as a result they always had food on the table. She had many things to be happy about. Every month, though, there was this empty ache in her soul. Sometimes a quiet ache, sometimes a severe ache: but it was an ache that never quite went away.

She watched little boys, running and shouting at their games, in the evening. She watched young girls, giggling and playing and watching everything that happened, seeking to understand the relationships between people. All these unique individuals, every single one of them was some mother's baby, every single one had grown in some mother's womb. But never, never, had a baby grown inside of her.

Years went by. Still no pregnancy.

At the end of a long summer afternoon, Sarai sat and watched the sun drop slowly into the west. She had come up with a plan. For the last two days she had been thinking of little else other than this plan. She did not think it was a good plan, but it was a plan that might yet get her what she wanted: and it had become obvious to her that continuing as they were would never succeed. So she felt the resolve growing stronger in her heart, despite her fears.

Aunt Sarai was pretty sure that in all their years together, Abram had loved only her. When he and his men had driven cattle to sell in a distant town, he obviously would have had opportunities to try out some of the harlots in those places: and if he told his men to say nothing about it when he did, of course they would obey him. Yet sooner or later those men would have let something slip in their pillow talk with their own women when they got home, and word would get around: it just does, for that sort of thing, even when people want to keep it quiet. Aunt Sarai had never heard any whisper of a rumor about this; and she had never detected any sign in Uncle Abram that he was guarding a careful secret that she must not find out. So she was pretty sure that in all those years, he never had slept with anyone but her.

When they had been in Egypt, they had bought and sold cattle and trade goods, and they had bought a number of slaves. They had bought a young slave girl, Hagar, seven years old, as a maid for Aunt Sarai. The girl had been bright and energetic, a quick learner and fast at running errands for her mistress.

Now, ten years later, the girl had grown to be a young woman of seventeen. She was beautiful, and full of intelligence and wit. Sometimes there was a misty look in her eye, like she was gazing at something astonishing and good, something Aunt Sarai could not see. Yet with the eyes of long-lived wisdom Aunt Sarai knew well what a look like that means, on the face of a nubile girl: it meant that it was time for Aunt Sarai to arrange a marriage for her slave.

She had known it would be necessary, but she did not want to do it. She could of course set it up so that Hagar became the wife of one of the young herdsmen; it would not be necessary to send Hagar to a husband outside their household. Still, even if she got a husband for Hagar and kept her as a servant, it would mean that the girl would no longer be constantly at Aunt Sarai's beck and call, but would be caring for her own husband and children some of the time.

Her own children. That was the sticking point. Something in Aunt Sarai's soul could not quite get over the resentment at the thought that it was her responsibility to set up a marriage for her slave girl and one of the marriageable slave boys, so that those two teenagers could start having babies, while she herself continued childless.

And so Aunt Sarai reached her decision. As the dusk deepened after supper that evening, Aunt Sarai stood with Uncle Abram at the front door of the master tent. She called Hagar to her, and the girl ran up, almost dancelike in the movements of her young womanly grace. Aunt Sarai held each of them by the hand, and said, "Abram my husband: I give you Hagar, my slave, as concubine. May she bear children, my children, in my name."

Both Uncle Abram and Aunt Hagar were shocked, of course. It was plain to see on their faces. Uncle Abram was 85 that year, but still vigorous; and in his mind he suddenly looked at Hagar as a beautiful girl in his bed, and not simply as just another of the many slaves and servants that looked after the running of his property. He did his best to make his face impassive, as if he could only consider such an action because his beloved wife asked him to do it, and would take no pleasure in it for himself; but he could not completely hide the fact that after all these years of faithfulness to one aging woman, he was about to have sex with this teenage girl, and he was thinking about what that would be like. Aunt Sarai read that look on his face, and it made her soul quail: but she had made her decision, and she would not stop now.

For her part, Aunt Hagar was also trying very hard not to react at all; yet she could not quite keep her lip from quivering. She had secretly been pining for a particular boy among the not-yet-attached young bucks in Uncle Abram's household. She knew that as an Egyptian slave girl among this family, she had no status at all. Those three reasons—Egyptian, slave, girl—added up to the reality that she could not possibly insist on her own choice for husband. Indeed, she would probably never even be asked if she had a preference. Still, she had felt sure that her mistress would assign her to one or another of the boys her own age. Hagar tried not to move at all, not a gesture of a hand nor any movement of her face: she dared not let her emotions show, at a moment like this. She knew she truly respected Uncle Abram with all the veneration he was due as master of the household, but he was so old! In all her seventeen-year-old-girl dreams of what sex and babies and family would mean, she had never imagined that she would be given as concubine to a man 85 years old!

But she could not reveal that. Aunt Sarai had spoken with a finality that could not be opposed. Aunt Hagar knew she should smile, she should thank her mistress, she should pretend that she felt so greatly honored by this: but she felt so afraid of expressing any emotion at all. Her soul was screaming: *No, no, no! Don't make me do this, please, please!* She clamped her jaw. She knew that if she said any such thing, it would be a disaster for her. It would mean at least a serious beating. At least that, and maybe much worse. As a slave of such low status, if she were to indicate reluctance to be bedded by her master, that would be such a grave insult. Who knew how terrible the punishment might turn out to be? She could be sold as a brothel slave. She could be beaten so severely that she would be crippled for life. She could be whipped till her skin was ripped to bloody rags, and then left to die. Such things happened to slaves all the time. So Aunt Hagar was afraid to move, lest she reveal what she was thinking. She did her best not even to breathe: and then she simply nodded once and then looked down at the ground, hoping it would look as if she were embarrassed, too shy to look up at them anymore.

Neither Uncle Abram nor Aunt Sarai noticed any of this, for they were looking at each other. Then Aunt Sarai drew her hands together, and placed Aunt Hagar's hand in Uncle Abram's. She set her hands on the shoulder of each of them, and pushed them toward the door of the master tent.

So it was that Uncle Abram and Aunt Hagar spent a honeymoon week in the master tent. Aunt Sarai, sleeping alone in her own small tent, ten paces off to the side, did her best not to listen to the sounds of the night. She had kept her health and her figure and her looks remarkably well, for a woman of 75, and she knew that Abram still praised her beauty when they made love: but she also knew that in terms of raw sexual attractiveness she could not compare to the vivid youthful beauty of Hagar. Her confidence in her husband was strong; she was very sure that his loyalty to her meant that he would never on his own have decided to sleep with this young girl. But now she, Sarai, had made it happen. She understood how men feel about sex: and she could not escape the dread in her soul that Abram might decide he really liked Hagar as an energetic young bedmate, and was going to keep her there with him from now on, with Sarai relegated to being just another old woman in the household. Each night as she heard the sounds of lovemaking from the adjacent tent, she wept in silence and in fear.

At the end of the week, Uncle Abram sent Aunt Hagar back to her own tent, and called Aunt Sarai back to the master tent once again. Aunt Sarai longed to ask about Uncle Abram's week with Hagar, but she was pretty sure she would be snippy about it, and she knew that bitter words would not help her cause. Uncle Abram wanted to offer her words of reassurance, but he could not figure out how to do it without talking about the fact that he had just spent a week having sex with someone other than Aunt Sarai. And so neither of them ever spoke to each other about that week. Instead, they did their best, with habitual words and gestures, to offer one another the reassurance that they were still the devoted couple that they had been for so long. And they tried not to think about the fact that it might take several months of this, before Hagar would conceive.

As for Aunt Hagar herself: being naked in the bed of the old man, and seeing him naked in bed beside her, had been so strange and embarrassing. It was not repulsive, exactly, but she had certainly felt severely awkward about it, at first. But the old man had turned out to be compassionate and gentle, and he had understood that she was full of anxieties and objections that she was too scared to express. When he had seen the tears welling up in her eyes, tears he could see she was trying to prevent but not succeeding, he had not only let her cry, but had held her calmly and comfortingly in his strong arms while she did. And it seems that he had learned many secrets about awakening desire, through the long years of his marriage, and he had used those caresses so well that Aunt Hagar was caught off guard at the ardor of her body's response. She had not expected that she would enjoy Uncle Abram's efforts to impregnate her, and yet she had. Even now she certainly did not expect she could ever really fall in love with someone so much older than herself; but the compassion and respect and cherishing that he had given her still felt more like love than anything she could remember, in all her ten years since leaving Egypt.

When her time came at the end of that month, Hagar did not bleed. She waited a couple of extra days, thinking she might just be a little late this month; but there was no blood. She wanted to wait another month before she told anyone, just to be sure. Partly this was because she had heard too many stories of women who thought they were pregnant and rejoiced as they told everyone, and then were embarrassed when they discovered a week or ten days later that they were not pregnant after all. But there was more. "If Abram and Sarai think I have not yet conceived," she said to herself, "then I will get to spend another week in bed with the master." That realization surprised her, but there it was. Considered as an abstract idea, it still seemed quite weird that she would be naked in bed with an 85-year-old man. Yet her body didn't seem to care about that: her body was craving to be held and touched and caressed by him again.

A few days later, just before supper one evening, Aunt Sarai asked her quite directly. Hagar could not lie to her: she could only say that her period had not come and she thought she might indeed be pregnant. Something happened in that moment, when Hagar spoke the words out loud: something that had not happened, up till that point, as long as it had only been in the quiet of her own mind that she had been thinking about what it might mean. When she had said out loud "I think I might be pregnant," she felt a wonder and delight bubbling forth within her, at the prospect of bringing a new life into this world. The words burst forth from her soul: "I'm going to be a mother! I'm going to have a baby!"

What was Aunt Hagar feeling at that moment? Perhaps it was just astonishment as she accepted that this pregnancy was a reality. Perhaps it was pride in thinking that she was becoming a mother: and perhaps it was even pride that she had managed to do something that her mistress had never done. It was, in any case, a strong emotion: and Aunt Sarai heard that strong emotion in Hagar's voice, and to her ears it sounded like haughtiness and contempt. It sounded as if Hagar suddenly thought she was something special, and indeed superior to her mistress. Aunt Sarai flew into a rage. Who did this impudent little Egyptian slave girl think she was? Why, she'd been a nothing all her life, and Aunt Sarai had owned her these last ten years since the brat was just seven, and now that this hussy had conceived a child she thought she was the queen of the world, and better than her mistress. Well! We'll just see about that!

Aunt Sarai was a woman of deep wisdom well-earned across seventy-five years of life, yet in that moment she could not look at the situation dispassionately enough to recall that she herself was the one, after all, who had established this surrogate mother setup in the first place, in the hope that it would have exactly this result. She could not recognize, in that moment, that Hagar's astonished outburst of emotion over this pregnancy was pretty much the same excitement that expectant mothers have felt since the dawn of time. She could not see past the turmoil in her own soul, in that moment, to acknowledge that of course Hagar, still scarcely more than a child herself, would not at the age of seventeen have developed the mature insight she would need to discern that her mistress might react badly to too much enthusiasm about this pregnancy; Hagar would not be able to see that it would be best to curb her own emotions and to speak to her mistress in an especially submissive tone of voice.

All those wise possibilities were of no avail, in that moment. All was rage, as Aunt Sarai went screaming to Uncle Abram: "This is all your fault! I pray God that this pain will land on your head, because after I gave my slave girl to your embrace and she got herself pregnant, she is getting all uppity and is looking at me with contempt. May God judge in my favor, and lay the blame on you!"

Uncle Abram was baffled by this outburst. What had he done, other than to follow his wife's own request, sleep with the girl in hopes that she'd get pregnant, which apparently now had happened? He felt like he had walked in on the middle of an argument, having missed the beginning, and he was pretty sure that it would be a losing strategy to try to catch up by having her review where all the conversation had been that had led up to all this distress. He felt like the best he could do was to make it clear that it was up to her to handle the situation in whatever way she thought best. So that's what he said: "She's your slave, you have the power to do whatever you feel like you need to do."

Then Aunt Sarai went storming back to the tent where Hagar sat, desolately weeping. Hagar's soul had jumped from hesitant possibility to astonished gladness to fearful trembling, all in a few minutes: and now she was too scared to know what to think or do. Aunt Sarai stood before her, pointing her finger and shouting, "Get out! Get out of my tent, get out of my sight, you miserable little wretch!" Aunt Sarai grabbed a broom and swung it at Hagar's head. The girl got her arm up part way and caught the blow on the point of her elbow, and she felt her whole forearm and hand go numb as she scrambled out the door of the tent. She ran into the middle of the camp, with Aunt Sarai chasing after her, waving the broom and screaming curses. Hagar looked around at the other slaves for help, but they all turned away, making themselves busy with whatever unimportant project they found close at hand. Then Aunt Sarai caught up with her again, swinging her broom and smacking it across Hagar's backside. She yelped in pain, and looked at Uncle Abram in desperation, but he carefully did not look at her. Aunt Sarai swung again and broke the broomstick across Hagar's shoulder blade. Hagar was wailing with pain by now, pleading, "Please stop, mistress, please don't hit me, please stop!" But Aunt Sarai simply threw the broken broom handle on the ground. She looked around, and saw a shovel in the hands of one of the servants, and scurried across to grab it away from him. As she turned back toward Hagar, waving the shovel, the girl summoned the courage of desperation to run out of the camp and into the desert with nothing but the clothes on her back. Aunt Sarai chased her into the twilight. In just a few dozen paces, though, the darkness had swallowed up the fleeing girl, and Aunt Sarai used her remaining breath to scream after her: "Get out! Get out! Get out!"

That night, Aunt Sarai sat in quiet shame, looking at the folded blanket tucked in the empty corner where Hagar ordinarily sat when she had no task immediately at hand. Aunt Sarai's rage had evaporated. All the wisdom and experience that had failed her that afternoon had returned, and she saw that whatever immaturity of emotion Hagar the teenager might have expressed, nearly all the blame for nearly all the immaturity fell squarely on Aunt Sarai's own shoulders. Aunt Sarai would have claimed to be the one who was actually all grown up; but she certainly had not acted the part.

And Aunt Hagar did not come back that night. It was cold in the desert night, and she was hungry and thirsty, bruised and scared and alone, but she did not come back. She knew there was a spring, a day's journey south of the camp, and first by the fading light in the west, then by the light of the gibbous moon when it arose, she ran and walked and ran some more, her feet and legs and shoulder aching so badly. She just wanted to collapse on the ground and wrap her arms around her knees and cry for an hour, but she knew she could not stop: on and on she had to keep going, no matter how ragged her pace, because she had to reach that spring by dawn. The grey sky in the east had turned to orange when she arrived, and she fell on her face at the edge of the spring. And she thought that no water could ever have tasted so fine.

When she had drunk her fill and her weary gasps of breath had returned to normal once again, Hagar twisted herself around and put her feet in the spring, and scooped up water to ease her bruises and wash away the dried blood. Then she slept, heedless of the hard ground and the heat of the day. She had lain down in a spot that was shaded by the scrubby trees growing there. Several times during the day she woke up, feeling the intensity of the sun's heat when the shade had moved away; each time she crawled back into the shade, and fell asleep again.

Late in the afternoon, she finally climbed to her feet. Every movement ached. She got a drink from the spring. There were some grasses growing, near the water, with their seed heads bobbing occasionally in the fitful breeze. Hagar reached over and pulled half a dozen stalks out of the ground, and rubbed the seed heads between her palms to work the seeds loose. In a minute she had a small handful of raw grain, and she put it in her mouth, chewing it slowly and steadily. It didn't taste like much of anything, but it was real food, and she could feel the strength of it within her. She pulled another half dozen stalks, and did it again. And as she chewed, she thought.

She had no food or water to sustain herself. She had no weapon to defend herself. She had no money to provide for herself, if she were to come upon a village or a caravan from whom she might have bought supplies. She had just the poor clothing of a slave girl, nothing more.

Here she was, out in the wild, on her own for nearly a day now. She felt the edges of panic, realizing how very precarious her situation was. She could be attacked by a wild lion or bear, animals she could neither outrun nor outfight, and she would be dead, no doubt about it. She could encounter a band of marauders, which would mean a rough gang rape and then being left stripped and bleeding to death into the desert sand. Or she could just die of hunger or thirst, and the birds and bugs would eat her flesh and leave nothing but dry bones in the wilderness.

Yet at the same time, she also felt a ferocious sense of exultant pride. She had survived, on her own, in the wilderness for a night and a day, despite having fled with nothing at all to help sustain her. And she would continue to survive. She would . . . she would go to Egypt! That's it, she thought with sudden resolve. She would go to Egypt, she and her unborn child, that's where they would go, and they would survive all the way there. If she could make steady progress, if nothing went wrong, it would take her two or three weeks of steady walking to get there. Maybe she could find her family; she could not remember very many names from her childhood, but she could remember a few, and if she could find even one relative, that would probably be enough to get her started: they would provide some kind of home for her and her baby. Even if she couldn't find any relatives, she still might be able to make a life for the baby and herself there.

In any case, it was clear there was no life for her in the wilderness. Nor could she go back to Sarai. Even though Sarai her mistress was the one who had decided that Hagar was supposed to be a mother, it was clear there was no life for her in going back and trying to be a good and obedient slave again: not after Aunt Sarai had chased her away with such fierceness: "Get out! Get out!"

"All right," said Aunt Hagar. "I am going to survive all the way to Egypt, or else I am going to perish on the way: but live or die, that's where I am going."

The sun was low in the west, and so Hagar hurried to search the ground around the spring until she found a stone of the shape she needed; oblong, large enough to fit comfortably in her hand, broken on one end to form an edge. She found another rock to strike it with, and chipped away at that edge to form a crude stone knife. With her knife she cut a wide piece of cloth from the hem of her garment; then she cut a piece off the end of that, and split it into two strips for tie cloths. She gathered the corners of the large piece, to form a pouch. Then, with the sun dipping toward the horizon, she pulled every stalk of grass from around the spring of water, and rubbed every single grain loose from the seed heads, and put that grain in her makeshift pouch. With one of her ties she tied her makeshift grain pouch to the left side of her belt, and with the other she tied her stone knife on the right.

Then she knelt down and drank and drank and drank, until she felt like she could hold no more: and then simply sat, with her back leaning against one of the trees, and waited. She waited until it was fully dark, stretching her legs some, but mostly just deliberately resting. She could hear night animals moving around. The previous night Aunt Hagar had simply run, not listening or caring: but now, as she sat quietly listening, she could hear the night animals, and it worried her as she thought about what predators there might be, close enough to be hunting those animals, close enough to be hunting her. Still she waited, quietly, until the moon rose; and then she knelt yet once more at the spring, and forced herself to drink to the point of discomfort: and then she headed south, hiking steadily under the cool desert moon.

It was a hard journey. Even though ordinarily the family usually traveled by day, as did any caravan, she knew that she needed to travel only at night: with no supplies of food or water to sustain her, she knew she could not live through a day of traveling in the heat of the desert sun. During the day she mostly slept, burrowing into whatever shade was available, doing her best to stay cool and to preserve her stamina. The moon rose later each night, and so the time when there was sufficient light for her to keep a steady walking pace, between moonrise and dawn, decreased each day: she knew that she was making a little less progress, from one night to the next. She could feel that her strength was decreasing as well. At the end of each night's march, as she began to look for a spring of water in the light of the rising sun, she thought again that this was the weariest she had ever been in her entire life: and then the following day, as the sun came up, she thought, "No, right now I am even more worn down than I was yesterday."

The thing she wanted to do in the dawn's early light was simply to collapse; yet she knew that the first thing she had to do by morning's light was to find water, because that was the difference between life and death: two or three scrubby trees, probably hidden down in a ravine, indicating the trickle of a brook or at least the seepage of a tiny spring. Often she could find it in the first glow of dawn, before the sun had fully risen above the horizon; but there were several days when Aunt Hagar had to press on for another hour into the morning's gathering heat, in order to find the water that would keep her alive for another day.

When she found it, she would drink and drink, and then sleep, waking only to drink some more and then crawl over to wherever the shade had moved to, so she could sleep some more. Late in the afternoon she would forage, gathering every single stalk of grass, rubbing out the seeds, eating half and putting half in her grain pouch to chew on when she sat to rest for a brief period in the middle of the night.

Then one morning she could not find water at all. She walked another hour, and then another, desperately hoping that over the next rise she might spot some small leafy branch reaching above the walls of a ravine, or some rough bushes gathered in a small crevice, some sign of a spring somewhere: but she could find none at all, nothing but rocks and sand. She nearly made the fatal mistake of pushing herself to keep on going, despite the blazing heat. But her eye spotted a shadow of darkness, part way up a hill: a small cave. She crawled inside. It was dry, and blessedly cool. It was not a comfortable place: the cave was cramped and short and there was a rock that pressed against her hip at an uncomfortable angle; yet she was too far gone for any discomfort to keep her from falling into the depths of exhausted sleep.

When darkness came she revived enough to crawl with painful slowness out of the cave, weary, parched, feeling gritty and at the edge of despair. It would be many hours before the moon would rise, but she started out in the darkness under the stars anyway, moving slowly, resting often, knowing she was at the last limits of her strength and must find water or die. Deep in the middle of the night, the moon finally rose. By then Hagar had fallen many times, and through the pain of each successive fall she had felt the sureness that death was very near, and all she needed to do was slip off into sleep and wait for dawn to come and finish her. Yet each time somehow she had managed to drag herself back onto her feet once again, and continue. In the pale light of the waning crescent moon, she plodded along, forcing herself to stagger along, forcing herself to look up, to look around: and she spotted the ragged grove of trees, off to the side, and with the last shreds of her resolution she limped those last hundred paces, and found the small trickle of water that meant she would live.

She stayed there the rest of that night; and all the next day and night as well. She had never felt so tired, and she wanted at least some of that deep aching weariness to go away. More than that, she wanted the fear to go away. Underneath the physical pain of thirst and exhaustion, she had felt so scared that she was about to die there in the desert: and those tremors of fear had not yet gone away. When she thought about another night of marching in the desert, the anticipatory fear was nearly overwhelming: what if there was no spring to be found, and so she would just finally fall in the desert and die? Or what if there would be a spring but her eyes would be so dim with exhaustion that she would miss it? So she remained there through a second full day, resting and foraging, hoping that she would awaken from a long afternoon nap and feel strong and vibrant and ready to walk again.

Because Egypt was near. She thought maybe two more days, and she would be in the wilderness of Shur, just at the edge of Egypt. There was water there, and she would be safe; and after that she would be in populated country, and could begin to ask questions that might lead her to her family. She was almost there: she had almost made it. She needed to find the strength for two more nights of walking, and she needed to find a spring of water where she could rest, between those two nights: and then she would be free, and alive, and ready to face whatever life in Egypt might bring. So when she woke up, late in the afternoon, she gathered her pouch and her stone knife and knelt at the spring to drink her fill once again.

That's when the angel showed up.

Aunt Hagar had never seen an angel before; and indeed, most of us never have. Angels always seem to come as a surprise; they never call to make an appointment first. They just appear, and your life gets rearranged in ways you never could have predicted.

Aunt Hagar was frightened, of course, but she was far too tired to try to run away, and in any case you could never run fast enough to get away from an angel. The angel called her by name: "Hagar, slave-girl of Sarai, where have you come from and where are you going?"

It seemed like kind of an odd question. The angel plainly knew who she was, both by name and also by occupation and owner; you would think that any angel who knew all that would also know where she had come from and where she was going. Throughout the generations, though, our people have had many occasions where God presents to us a question that requires a response. We have discovered it is not because God needs the information and is hoping that we will provide the answer; instead, God asks us such questions because we need the chance to express the truth of the answer out loud, and hear it coming from our own mouth. Perhaps that was what was happening, with Aunt Hagar. In any case, she saw no advantage in lying: and so she simply said, "I am running away from my mistress Sarai."

The angel said, "Go back to your mistress, and submit to her."

The weight of this command settled onto Aunt Hagar's shoulders and tightened around her chest, pressing the air from her lungs, heavier than a great load of firewood, heavier than a severe beating, heavier than sin. She was so close! After so many nights of steady pacing, so many times falling and getting bruised and struggling back to her feet once again, after all the thirst and exhaustion, after so nearly dying three nights ago, she was almost there, just a couple days from the border of Egypt, just two days from the beginning of a new life. And now, *now* she had to go back to her mistress?

I suppose she might have refused, and gone on to Egypt anyway. People disobey God's word quite often; they shrug off a command from God as if one more instance of disobedience could hardly matter. Then again, Aunt Hagar might simply have given up, lying down and never getting up again, simply overcome by this word of the Lord: unable to contemplate the possibility of doing the whole journey over again, twenty more days of walking through the desert, this time in the opposite direction.

The angel went on: "You are indeed pregnant, and you will have a baby boy. You are to give him the name Ishmael"—which means *God hears*—"because the Lord has heard your distress. Your son will grow up to be a wild man; it will seem like everyone is against him, and even his kinfolk will look at him with hostility."

This was not the most favorable prophecy over a child that anyone could ever imagine. Yet Aunt Hagar found the beginnings of hope growing in her soul, as she listened to it. God Almighty had spoken to her, in the form of this messenger: face to face with God she had heard this message, and yet she was not blotted out. She had seen God, and God had seen her: not from a great distance, but close enough to shake hands. The word that God had spoken was difficult: difficult to hear, difficult to obey. Still, life itself was difficult, and always had been, for Aunt Hagar. All her days she had known that life would never be easy.

Somehow she found her voice enough to respond. "You are the God who sees me," she acknowledged. It was not many words, to speak face to face with God: but it was about all she could do in that moment, and somehow it expressed her decision that she would indeed do what the God who sees her told her to do. In God's honor she gave a name to this spring where she had encountered God: Be'er-lahai-roi, "The Spring of the Living One Who Sees Me." The journey ahead of her would be hard, and her life on the other side of that journey would be hard: but she had seen God, and she knew the reality of God's call to her would sustain her.

So Aunt Hagar made her way, slowly and steadily, back to the household of Uncle Abram. She kept looking around for the angel, on the return trip; several times she felt like someone was watching over her, but she never actually saw anyone. Maybe she had built up her endurance a little better, or maybe she just didn't push herself to be in so much of a hurry, but she felt less wearied on her way back; and then it rained, so there were brooks and pools of water in many places, and they were not hard to find. Soon enough she came to the familiar region where Uncle Abram's camp had been, and then she encountered a group of Uncle Abram's shepherds, with one of the flocks. They gave her directions toward the camp: and a few hours later the tents were in sight, and then she had walked into the center of the campsite itself.

There was no exuberant homecoming. Aunt Sarai did not run up to her and welcome her back with a big hug. She only managed to say, "I am glad you are all right. And I am glad you are back." Soon Aunt Hagar had settled in once more to her life as Aunt Sarai's slave.

They were curious about how she had managed, during her six weeks in the wilderness. Aunt Hagar never said much about that. But she did tell the story of the angel that had met her at the spring in the wilderness, and how the angel had said that the baby should be named

Ishmael, because God Hears. She told how she had given that spring of water a special name: the Spring of the Living One Who Sees Me. And in due time she brought forth a son. Uncle Abram gave him the name Ishmael, in obedience to the word that God had spoken to Hagar.

So Uncle Abram and Aunt Sarai now had a son, borne by Aunt Hagar. It seemed that the details of the story were lining up nicely for a happy ending—or at least one with a fair measure of contentment, as one generation saw the next generation running around, growing and playing and laughing.

Then it came to pass, when Uncle Ishmael had become a young teenager, God appeared to Uncle Abram once again. God reaffirmed his covenant with Uncle Abram and Aunt Sarai, giving them new names: Abraham and Sarah. And he gave Abraham and Sarah the promise that they would have their own child.

Abraham laughed at this. "I am nearly a hundred years old now," he said to himself. "Sarah will be ninety, on her next birthday. We both are much healthier than anyone has a right to expect: we walk and work without pain, we can move the campsite to another place whenever we wish to, we even still make love: and we do these things at an age when all our contemporaries—and most of their children—are long since dead. I am grateful for all these blessings. But surely it is too late to expect that we will get a child of our own."

What had come to pass, for Uncle Abraham and Aunt Sarah, was that they had grown content in their own age as they watched young Ishmael's childhood unfolding before them. He was a fine energetic youth, full of life and vigor. Knowing that he would take their name and their heritage to the next generation brought deep happiness to them both.

Yet God had something else in mind. "Next year at this time," said God, "Sarah will be cradling her own son in her arms."

Sarah was listening at the door of the tent, and she heard this, and she laughed too. "Ah, what a miracle that would be," she thought, not believing it could ever be. "I am so long past the age of childbearing: such a delight it would be, but I know this delight will never be mine."

God spoke up, and asked, "Why did Sarah laugh? Do you think this would be too hard a miracle for God to be able to do such a thing?"

Aunt Sarah was afraid she might be in trouble: so she denied it at once, "No, no, I didn't laugh, it was just . . . something caught in my throat." It was not, indeed, that she thought that God could not do it; it was simply that God had not done it—and had not done it, and had not done it—throughout all the decades when she had hoped and prayed and yearned for the birth of her own child, and God had not done it in all those years. Surely it had never been too hard a miracle for God any time in all those long years of frustration.

"And yet, you did laugh," said God.

That might seem as if God were angry that she had laughed: perhaps angry enough that now the miracle would not happen. But the miracle did happen. A year later, Aunt Sarah had a child, her own son, and they named him Isaac, which means *laughter*: a remembrance of the laughter of Abraham and the laughter of Sarah when they listened to God's promise, and the laughter and joy the two of them shared as they held this newborn in their arms.

So now there were two sons growing up in this family: Uncle Ishmael, the son of Aunt Hagar, about fourteen years older than Uncle Isaac, the son of Aunt Sarah. One day, when Uncle Isaac was about three years old, Aunt Sarah saw the two boys playing. Uncle Ishmael was nearly 17, and her boy Isaac looked up at his big brother with such devotion: and in that moment Aunt Sarah knew that Ishmael had to go. Her son was the true son. Ishmael was nothing more than the son of a slave. And yet because Ishmael was so much older, her Isaac followed Ishmael around as if he were the true leader. That had to stop. And that meant Ishmael and his mother had to go.

The more Aunt Sarah thought about this, the madder it made her: and so when she broached the subject with Uncle Abraham, she was quite insistent: "Tell this slave woman and her son to get out, for the son of this slave woman shall not inherit along with my son Isaac!" Uncle Abraham found this quite distressing; yet, when he prayed over this matter, God told him, "Don't be anxious: just do whatever your wife tells you to do. Indeed, it will be through Isaac that your descendants will be named for you. But Ishmael also will be a mighty nation."

And so Aunt Hagar found herself once again in the desert. This time she had some food and a leather bottle of water, provided by Uncle Abraham. This time she was not pregnant, but accompanied by a teenage son. This time she was not herself a teenager, but a woman in her thirties.

She knew how to survive in the desert: but she also knew how hard it is to survive in the desert. She remembered the last time she had been alone in the desert, and all of that great aching fear came flooding back into her soul. She had been so scared that she was about to die, and now she could feel that same fear that she and her son were going to die. It was the middle of the day. There was no shade. They trudged along. Soon the water bottle was empty. Ishmael was young and strong, but the heat was overwhelming him, and soon he was staggering, leaning on his mother, and finally she could not support his weight any longer. There was a low scrubby desert bush, withered, no more than half her height, and she let him fall to the ground underneath it. It was only partial shade, and his feet still stuck out into the full sun, but it was all there was.

She didn't know what to do. She hobbled along another hundred paces until she came to a desert boulder that provided another tiny patch of shade, and sat down in it. "I can't bear to watch him die," she said to herself. "O God," she wept, "why have you let it come to this? You told me to name the boy Ishmael, because '*God hears*.' And is that still true? Do you still hear me?"

And indeed Aunt Hagar found that it is still true that God hears. The God who hears heard the gasping of Ishmael. The Living One who sees saw the tears of Hagar. The voice of Lord called to Aunt Hagar: "Do not be afraid. That boy will yet become a great nation. Fill the water bottle at the spring and get him a drink. He'll be just fine."

She looked around in wonder: and there she saw a spring of water. Had it been there all along, and she had failed to see it? Or had God brought that spring into being, just at that moment? She could not tell. It did not matter. She staggered to the spring, filled the water bottle, and brought some to Uncle Ishmael. He drank it, and felt restored.

They survived in the desert, Aunt Hagar and her son, Uncle Ishmael. They journeyed to Egypt, and she found a wife for him there. But they did not feel at home, in Egypt, and they moved back to the desert again, and there they lived as nomads.

The story of Aunt Hagar is mostly forgotten: yet it is a story that we would do well to remember. It is the story of someone whose voice seemed doomed never to be heard: for with three strikes against her—Egyptian, slave, girl—why would anyone ever bother to listen to her? And yet she is the one who comes to know, despite great adversity, that God hears and God sees. That is our family's heritage. We are people who have come to know that God hears and God sees. Aunt Hagar is the one who taught us that.

6

From the Mists of Eden

ONCE UPON A TIME, long ago when I was a small boy seven years old, on a Friday afternoon in late summer, I asked my great-grandmother a question.

Her name was Miriam, but everyone called her Aunt Miriam. As I've mentioned, in our extended family everyone is Aunt this or Uncle that; but with Aunt Miriam everyone called her this, not only people in our family. Other people in our town, and places round about as well: everyone called her Aunt Miriam. She was like a sage or something, a person of wisdom, and people would come to ask her questions: to settle disputes, sometimes, or to gain a better understanding of one of the riddles of life. Even though she was my great-grandmother, I called her Aunt Miriam just like everyone else did. It was impossible to call her anything else. (One time as a teenager I had decided I was going to call her Great-grandma. It didn't work. I looked at her and tried to say, "Great-grandma," and what came out was, "Aunt Miriam.")

I had come to her to ask my question, that Friday, because three days earlier, on Tuesday, I had been bad. There was a pear tree in the back yard of a neighboring family; and the pears on this tree had been steadily ripening. There was no doubt in my mind that to steal pears from their pear tree would be wrong. It would be sin. That was how we talked back then. People nowadays do not ordinarily identify their wrongdoing as *sins*; instead, we say things about juvenile pranks or about making inappropriate choices. But we did not talk that way back then. The things you did wrong were sins.

I had sinned. I had crept into the neighbors' yard and taken two pears from the tree. I had, I thought, been very careful in my sneakiness so that no one could have seen me. I ate those pears. The first was so fine: full of juice and flavor, spiced with the guilty delight in a successful criminal score. The second was not so fine: somehow its texture seemed more mealy, its flavor not quite so sweet, and the guilt felt less spicy and more heavy.

"Be sure your sin will find you out," as Uncle Moses said long ago, and this word of the Lord certainly came to fulfillment in my case. My father learned of my transgression from the neighbors, and justice had been swift and sure. As the judgment drew near, I progressed rapidly through the stages: first Denial, then Bargaining, and then Anger (with loud and painful wails at first, which then eventually subsided into mumbled sulking some time after the rod of judgment had landed on my backside). Then, surprisingly, came Acceptance. It was indeed true that I had stolen the pears. It was clear to me that I deserved to be punished for it. Although I did not enjoy the punishment, in my soul I could acknowledge that it was just. Thus it was that I arrived, perhaps for the first time in my life, at genuine Repentance.

I was sorry that I had stolen the pears; but it was more than that. I had recognized, somehow, that there was something wrong in the depths of me. I had not failed because of ignorance. I had not sinned through inattention or accident. I had known it would be wrong to take those pears: but I wanted to do it, and I went ahead and did it. Now I wanted to know why it was that I had this wrong thing in the depths of me, and what I should do about it.

Thus it came to pass, on this particular Friday afternoon, I came as a repentant soul to my great grandmother to ask my question: "Aunt Miriam, why do I sin?"

She turned in her chair and looked at me. She smiled. She had so many great-grandchildren, I was never sure whether she could keep track of us all. Everyone called her Aunt Miriam: her own grandchildren and great-grandchildren, and parents and children in all the other families that lived nearby. How could she keep track of who was who? And yet, when Aunt Miriam smiled at you, you knew that that smile was for you.

Aunt Miriam smiled at me, and my heart warmed in the sureness that she loved me: but she did not say a word. She did not answer my question. But she did smile.

As children do, I would often blurt out the first thing that came into my head, and then feel embarrassed or ashamed about how my incautious words had revealed yet again some awkwardness of my being. But on this occasion, I did not blurt. I do not know why. Instead I stood there and responded with my own silence, as I pondered for a moment on Aunt Miriam's smile, and the warmth of her love.

An odd idea occurred to me, as I stood there waiting: *maybe the smile is the answer.* Maybe I don't need to have an explanation about why do I sin. Maybe all I really need is to feel the warmth in Aunt Miriam's smile, and to know that she loves me, and all my family loves me: and so I don't need to press for an answer in words. Maybe that's enough.

In that moment I felt a deep longing for that to be enough; I felt how wonderful it would be not to need any other explanation. To know that you are loved, sinner that you are: to know that the people who love you have decided that they will love you, forever, no matter what: maybe, just maybe, that can be enough. There may still be unanswered questions in your soul, and they may remain unanswered for all the time to come, and yet you can rest content to leave them unanswered: because you know that you are beloved. I felt it: I felt the longing deep within me, for the sureness of Aunt Miriam's love to be enough.

Yet even at age seven, that was not enough. At least, it was not enough for me. I think this may have been the first moment I realized how certain questions work. There are certain kinds of questions that, once you ask them, they are there and they won't go away. You could go along contendedly unaware that there could be a question about something; but if the day ever comes when you ask that question, you can never get yourself back to the point where you don't have that question. I know I could not have expressed that thought too well, at that age, but I saw it, even so. I knew that Aunt Miriam loved me, and that meant a lot: but it wasn't going to make this question go away.

So I had to ask again, "Aunt Miriam, why do I sin?" Maybe she did not know; although at age seven I believed that she knew everything. Maybe she would not tell me; I had discovered that grown-ups will not always tell you what you want to know. But I wanted to know this: I wanted to know! And the only way I might find out was to ask. "Aunt Miriam: why do I sin?"

This time she answered. She said, "Do you sin, my child?"

That caught me by surprise. Could it possibly be that she did not know about my most recent sin, stealing from the neighbor's pear tree? Immediately I saw that of course she knew. Everyone knew. Plus that was hardly my first sin ever. She could not be in doubt about the answer to that question. So why did she ask? Not in order to get information from me. But then, why did she ask? I did not know. So I remained silent.

She remained silent as well, for a long moment. She sat there, looking at me; and then I saw that she was not exactly looking at me, but more like looking inside me, into my soul; and then I saw that it was even more than that, she was looking right through my soul, as if my soul were a lens through which she could see into the mystery, the mystery of human life, the mystery of Why.

Let me tell you a story, she said. It is a story from so long ago, a story from deep in the mists of ancient days and passed down from generation to generation to generation, as so many stories are within our family. Once upon a time, you see, there was a young couple who had just gotten married. He was strong and handsome; she was beautiful, and the radiance in her eyes, when she spoke and when she listened and when she laughed in delight: the radiance in her eyes was so full of goodness and joy that it made the morning sunlight seem pale.

This young husband and wife: they loved each other very much. And God loved them, and blessed them. God gave them a home, and blessed them with a beautiful garden, full of flowers to delight the eye, and full of good food as well, to delight the tongue.

And each other! God had given them each other, and in the manner of young couples since the dawn of time, they found delight in each other's words, in each other's touch, in each other's love. They were blessed by God, and they were full of happiness.

Then one day the young woman looked out in the back yard and she saw a snake in the grass.

The snake said, "Hello."

And she replied, "Hello."

The snake said, "You know, your life isn't as happy as you think it is."

And she replied, "What makes you say that?"

The snake shrugged. "You can't have everything you want. How can you be happy if you can't have everything you want?"

She was surprised by all of this: surprised that a snake could shrug, surprised that a snake could talk, and surprised at the line the argument was taking. "I am happy," she said. "I have everything I want."

The snake said, "What about that tree?"

She knew which tree the snake meant. For God had said, "Anything in the garden you can eat for food. Except for this one tree, here in the middle: you may not eat the fruit of This One Tree. To eat from this tree is death."

So she knew that the snake's question "What about that tree?" did not refer to the olive tree or the fig tree. She knew it was about This One Tree: the tree that was called The Tree of the Knowledge of Good and Evil.

She told the snake, "We may not eat from that tree."

The snake said, "Oh, that's so sad. I have always heard that that is the very best tree in the whole garden: the fruit is the most delightful to the eyes, and yet it is even more delightful to the tongue. And that isn't even the best part."

The snake took a moment to look carefully to left and right to make sure there was no one close enough to overhear; and then leaned forward to whisper, "I have also heard that those who eat from that tree become full of knowledge: indeed, they become as wise as God." Then the snake leaned back once more, and tried to look innocent and noble. Then, after a moment's pause, the snake said ever so sincerely, "Well, never mind. If you can't have everything you want, then that's just the way it is. I guess it will have to be enough that you have some of those other, drab and boring things instead."

Then the snake slid away into the shrubbery and was seen no more.

The young woman felt a pang of longing in her soul, a longing for this forbidden fruit. How she wanted that fruit! She went to the tree—only to look at it, she told herself. The fruit seemed so ripe, so perfect; the aroma was so rich, so intoxicating, hanging there on the branch, calling to her. She had to taste it, she told herself. She just had to. And so she reached forth her hand and plucked it from the branch, and ate it.

Then she plucked another, and brought it to her husband. He took it from her hand. He looked at her, and knew that this was the fruit from The Tree of the Knowledge of Good and Evil, the one that God had said everything in the garden is for you, except that you must not partake from This One Tree—lest you die. And here it was, she had taken it! She had eaten it! And here she was, in front of him, still as radiant with laughter and delight as always: not dead at all. Indeed she seemed very alive, perhaps more alive than ever before, as if she knew some secret, as if she now held some knowledge that he could not guess at.

And he ate.

Suddenly they felt so ashamed. They had never felt that way before, and so they were afraid. This horrible depth of shame and fear was so painful, and they did not know what to do or how to get away from it: if only somehow they could hide themselves away and escape from it. And then they heard the voice of God.

God said, "What is this? Have you eaten from the tree that I commanded you not to eat from?"

The man said, "It wasn't me! It was her! She started it! She gave me some fruit from the tree, and I ate."

God turned to the woman: "What have you done?"

She answered, "I didn't do it! It was the snake! The snake tricked me! That's how the whole thing happened, that's why I did it."

Aunt Miriam had not really been looking at me while she told this story. I had been looking at her, looking at her face, looking at her eyes, and she had glanced back at me from time to time. Mostly, though, she had seemed to be looking somewhere far away, right through the wall and off to some misty distance I could not see, except through her words. Now she turned and looked directly at me, and said: "You asked 'Why do I sin?' Tell me then: why did the young woman sin?"

"That's easy," I blurted out. "Because the snake tricked her."

She looked at me. For a long moment she did not say anything. I still remember how nervous that made me, that long moment of silence.

Then she said, "You have not thought through your answer, child. But I give you permission to try again."

But I had no other answer to give. And so I simply repeated my previous words: "Because the snake tricked her."

"When you say *Because* the snake tricked her, does the *Because* mean that what the snake did forced her to sin? Was her sin caused by what the snake did, or by what she did?"

I almost blurted out, "What the snake did." But I paused instead, and thought about it, and then almost blurted out, "What she did." Yet I paused for another moment, and thought some more.

I think Aunt Miriam must have been able to read those almost-blurted answers on my face. She did not look impatient: she simply smiled with a smile that told me I could take all the time I needed to think it through.

Yet although I did my seven-year-old best to think hard, I could not figure out which answer to give; and so after a few moments I simply said, "I don't know."

She said, "Let me ask the question slightly differently. Why did the young woman take and eat the fruit from that tree?"

I thought about this. Then I said, "Because she wanted it."

She nodded at me. "And . . ."

I said, "And?"

"Which happened first? Did she take and eat it, and then find out she wanted it?"

"No. First she wanted it, and then she decided to take it."

Aunt Miriam said, "See what you have discovered here, my child. She wanted it, and then she decided to take it, and then she took and ate it."

I nodded.

"What about the snake?" asked Aunt Miriam. "The snake may have wanted to trick her. But did the snake's trickiness *make* her sin? Could she have ignored the snake, or laughed at the snake, or invited the snake to rejoice in the beauty of the flowers and sunshine and stop trying to be so tricky? Could she have done anything like that? Or was the snake's trickiness so clever that she really had no choice but to go ahead and eat the fruit?"

"I think the snake was very tricky," I said. "But I think she could have laughed at it, or ignored it. It didn't get bad for her until she went and looked at the tree again, and stood there thinking that she just had to have it."

Aunt Miriam said, "When was the sin? When she saw the fruit and found that she wanted it? Or when she decided to take it (but had not yet done so)? Or when she actually took it?"

I reflected on my recent experience with the pear tree. I felt ashamed. I wanted to run away and hide. Yet even in the middle of wanting to flee from being ashamed in front of Aunt Miriam, I saw something else. I could tell it was not by accident that the story she had decided to tell was about some people who had taken fruit that they were not supposed to take: she had chosen this story on purpose.

Still, I knew her purpose was not to shame me. I knew that, because I knew that Aunt Miriam loved me. I knew that even though I felt ashamed, it was not because of Aunt Miriam: she was not trying to make me feel bad, but teaching me the answer to the question I had started with: "Aunt Miriam, why do I sin?" And I still wanted to understand.

So I did not run away.

"It is all mixed up in my head," I said. "There was something wrong when I wanted to take the pears. There was something wrong when I sneaked into the yard. The wrongest was when I actually took and ate them."

"So," she said. "Can you tell me, now, why you took the pears?" I had known she was going to ask me that, and I had dreaded it; but there was no condemnation in her voice, no anger: simply the question, asked to give me an opportunity to answer.

"I don't know," I said. "It was wrong. I knew it. And I did it anyway."

She smiled at me, a smile of delight and encouragement and approval. "Yes," she said. "You have seen it. That is the insight, right there. Let me tell you this, my child, with the experience of a very old woman. There is no need to look for any explanation beyond that. Why did the young woman in the story sin? The sin was not caused by something outside herself: the cause was not the snake in the grass. The sin was caused by herself: she saw something she wanted, even though she knew it was wrong: but she decided to take it anyway, and then she did. Many of our sins are just like that. People see something they want, and so they decide to take it, and then they do. Their own decision is all the cause there is: they decide, and do. Do you understand that?"

I nodded.

Aunt Miriam nodded also. "Remember this lesson, then, my child. And answer me this further question. The young man in the story: why did he sin?"

"Because his wife told him to," I said. And yet even as I said it I could already see that it was not really the right answer.

Aunt Miriam's smile told me that she could see I was having second thoughts. She looked at me, and waited.

"I guess she didn't really tell him to," I said. "But it was like she was daring him: she had done it, and did he dare to do it too?"

Aunt Miriam nodded, but she said nothing, waiting for me to go on.

"And it was like he took the dare."

Aunt Miriam asked, "Did he have to take the dare?"

I pondered on this. It is very hard, when you are seven years old, not to take a dare. My friends and I would dare each other to do scary things: if someone dared you, you had to do it, because it was even scarier to think what they would say if you were afraid to take the dare. Still. I could see that nobody *makes* you take a dare.

"No," I said.

"So he could have declared, 'I won't do it!' and run away. Or he could have trembled and said 'You'll have to talk to God about this, I'm sure, and I'll go with you when you do that: but I don't know what you should say.' Or he could have said, 'Look, this isn't the right thing, we know that, let's just go do something else.' Is that right? Could he have done something different like that? Even though it was like she dared him to eat it?"

"Yes," I said. "It would have been hard. But he could have done something different."

"So, once again, my child. The sin was not caused by anything outside himself. What she did was kind of like daring him: but he did not sin because she dared him; he sinned because he made a choice. There is no need to look for any explanation beyond that. The sin was caused by himself: he saw what someone else did, and he went along and did it, too. Many of our sins are just like that. People see somebody else doing something wrong, it looks like they're getting away with it, and so they decide that they dare to do it too, and then they do. Once again, their own decision is all the cause there is: they decide, and do."

"But that's not what they said! In the story, I mean. In the story, he said it was her fault, and she said it was the snake's fault!"

"Indeed," said Aunt Miriam. "Were they telling the truth, when they said that?"

That stopped me. Were they lying? I had kind of assumed that if Aunt Miriam told me a story, every bit of it would have to be true: it could not contain any lies. And yet: what the man and woman had said wasn't really correct, was it? The story was a story about two people who had sinned, and then lied about it by putting the blame on others. I saw that, and my answer was almost a shout: "They were lying! They were lying, and blaming others for the things that they had done wrong!"

Aunt Miriam asked, "Were they lying?"

And I had no answer. All my confidence was gone, just that quickly: Aunt Miriam asked a question—not really to contradict me, but to give me a chance (as I later saw) to reconsider and perhaps reaffirm or perhaps modify what I had already said. Yet I could not answer at all. A moment earlier I had spoken with the total confidence of someone who suddenly sees with great clarity, as if there could be no question about what I had said: but as soon as any question was raised, everything was in doubt once more. And so I stood there, with no words I could offer in response.

Aunt Miriam said, "There are more possibilities here that you need to consider, child. Perhaps they were deliberately lying, and everything they said was false. Perhaps they were telling all the truth. But what else might it have been? Could they have been telling all the truth they knew (but there was other truth that they did not know)? Could they have been mistaken: they were not saying anything wrong on purpose, but they did not know that they were wrong about the things they were saying? Might they have been telling part of the truth, and holding something back because they were too embarrassed? Could they have been confused, because they had not really thought the thing through yet?"

I remember feeling overwhelmed by all these possibilities. I wanted to cry, actually: it all seemed way too hard.

At the same time, I felt a sense of hope. It was not yet contentment or assurance. I could not yet have stated for myself the answer to my question, "Why do I sin?" But somehow, somehow I was sensing that the answer I needed was in that story of the young husband and wife.

I had seen that my action, stealing the pears, had been like what the young woman had done. When you do that, when you see something you want and you know it's wrong but you do it anyway: well, that's how you sin. Even as a seven-year-old, I was getting this, thanks to Aunt Miriam's story; although it would still be many years before I could analyze this concept for myself, in any detailed way.

Yet I could already tell that the answer was in that story, in seeing how that story wasn't just about those two people, but about me. There were still lots of questions. I remember a very clear awareness of not-yet-understanding-the-whole-thing. Yet there was also a sense of peace: the peace of knowing that I was beloved, no matter what, and the peace of knowing that I had begun to understand the question "Why do I sin" by listening to the story of the young couple and the snake.

Aunt Miriam watched me working through this. Looking back on it all, I suppose that from many years of practice she was just very skilled in reading people's feelings from their faces and body language: though at the time it always seemed that she was looking into your soul and seeing what you were thinking as you thought your thoughts. It was clear that she had recognized that I had made my way from being at the point of tears to the beginnings of calm. Then she asked, "What have you learned?"

I said, "I am not sure."

Aunt Miriam smiled. "Ah, that is so fine. That is one of life's big lessons, my child: to be able to say, 'I am not sure.' Often a person can see the beginnings of things: an idea that can give you an insight, the start of an explanation. But it's just the beginning: it's not the whole explanation. You won't yet be sure what the whole thing means. The truth is, at that moment you won't yet even be sure what all the possibilities are; it will always take a little more time to consider what the other possibilities might be. And then you will have to take the time to go through all those possibilities, to try to figure out which possibilities might be right and which ones will turn out to be mistakes. You have learned a great deal, if you have learned to say, when you have a sudden insight, 'I am not sure.'"

In later years I wondered where Aunt Miriam got this story about the young couple and the snake. Did it come from some saga she had learned many years before, which she had then passed on to me? Or was it a story that she created, a parable she had made up right then in order to help a seven-year-old see why he sins?

I wish I had asked her that. Since then I have heard other versions of this same story, over the years. But Aunt Miriam died the winter I turned sixteen, and I had never asked her where her version came from.

7

The Story of the Do-Over Box

As my grandfather explained it to me, there was a big family reunion when his grandfather and grandmother were young newlyweds. Various branches of the family came from all over, for a gathering that would last for several days. There were more relatives than anybody could easily count, and they spent the time learning each other's names once again, and finding out about the youngsters and the oldsters. One evening they had a big barbecue and communal bonfire, with laughter and conversation, singing and dancing, and so much good food; and everyone stayed up late for the telling of many stories.

Our family has learned that it is in the remembering and retelling of stories that we recognize who we are. Some of the stories are told over and over again; some of them are only told once in a while. Some of the stories are funny, and some are sad; sometimes a member of our family is the hero, and sometimes it is a story where everything goes wrong. Some of these stories are quite brief, and some are quite long. We tell these stories, and we listen to them, and we find out that these stories which have been passed down in the family through long generations often turn out to be stories about ourselves in the here and now. Many of these stories are histories, remembering the relevant facts about what happened as closely as we can. Some of the stories we tell are parables, created by the story-teller to help us understand something about ourselves and our present situation, because we have learned that we find out who we are by telling stories.

Our family loves these stories. We tell them all the time. We learn who we are by listening to them. So on that night long ago, one of my grandfather's grandmother's uncles stood up and recounted this story. It was not actually the first time his grandmother had heard this story, but it was the first time she had heard it in this much detail: and it made quite an impression on her. Eventually she would tell the story to her children and grandchildren—and thus to my grandfather—and so it came eventually to me.

In the flickering light of that bonfire, all those years ago, that great-great-great-great-uncle told this story: and this is what he said.

* * * * *

The first thing I did when I woke up was to wish I hadn't. My tongue felt swollen, I felt bruised all over, and my eyes had been glued shut with some mixture of grit and gum. Somehow I managed to force them open. I could see. Kind of. Everything was blurred and dark.

Then my enemies saw that I was awake, and they started drumming on the top of my head with wooden sticks.

No.

They were pounding the inside of my head. Damn. The earlier hangovers had been bad, but this one was the worst ever.

I sat up, and hoped the spinning would stop before I ended up heaving. I hate to throw up. I know it's the body's normal reaction to something bad, and if you've swallowed something that has gone bad it's better to hurl it out, quickly. All the animals do it that way. But it's undignified and uncomfortable and I just hate it. So I sat there, trying to breathe slowly and deeply, and after a while the spinning ebbed away. But the enemies were still there, steadily pounding on the inside of my head.

The blanket had fallen away, and I could see that I was buck naked. Just how drunk did I get, last night, anyway? Drunk enough that I had spilled a hell of a lot of wine on myself; my chest was all sticky with the spills where I must have missed my mouth. The combined stink of old sweat and my own breath and stale spilled wine added up to too much, and the nausea came flooding back stronger than ever. I barely had enough time to turn my head so that the mess didn't land on the bed.

I realized I could see a little better—because the world had become a little more gray and a little less black—so I knew it was very early morning. Ha. Maybe I was puking drunk, but I had still awakened at my usual schedule, in the earliest pre-dawn twilight an hour or so before sunrise. I was always the first person awake in the morning, springing out of bed like a champion; and even though I didn't feel too springy right at the moment it looked like I was still going to be the first one up.

Because I was going to get up, in just another minute, anyway. As soon as the headache eased off a little. I did my breathing exercise again—slow inhale, hold; slow exhale, hold—and asked myself how I had gotten to bed last night, anyway. I could not recall. I shut my eyes and tried to review events. No good. I had no memory of it at all. I had apparently been quite the drunken sailor, and now here I was, by the dawn's early light, naked and stinking, hung over and throwing up, and no recollection of last night at all. What a mess.

I managed to stand up. I would not have believed the headache could have gotten more painful, but indeed it could; the enemies had either redoubled their efforts or invited in a few friends to help. But at least I was standing. Slow inhale, hold; slow exhale, hold. Do it again. I pulled on some clothes, and half-limped, half-staggered out the door.

It was not morning.

It was full dark night.

The moon had risen, a waning gibbous moon, four days past full and still bright enough to hurt my eyes. I closed my eyes—slow inhale, hold; slow exhale, hold—to give my brain a moment to catch up with reality: I had not awakened in the dawn's earliest light after all. It wasn't early morning; it was late evening, and I had gotten so wasted that I could not recall anything of what had happened, and then apparently had been passed out drunk all day long.

My eldest son had heard me, and had stepped out of his tent. "Dad," he said. "Are you all right?"

He handed me a cup of water, and I gulped it down. He took it away from me, refilled it, and handed it back, and I drained it again. He refilled it once more; I took a swallow, and sat down on the bench and closed my eyes for a moment—slow inhale, hold; slow exhale, hold—and then I was able to open my eyes and just sip at the water.

"This is pretty embarrassing," I said. "Just how big a fool did I make of myself?"

He sat down on the other end of the bench, not looking directly at me, obviously feeling awkward about the whole thing. "You were pretty drunk," he said.

"I guess I must have been," I nodded. "I do not remember any of it, till I woke up a few minutes ago. Apparently I did not jump right out of bed this morning."

"No," he said.

I could tell there was more. The enemy drummers were still there, but even through the headache I could see that his embarrassment had increased.

"Tell me," I said.

It was plain that he did not want to tell me.

"Well, we were all a little bleary-eyed when we got up this morning, and we were ready to go to work, but you didn't show up. We all felt kind of awkward about that, because you know we didn't really want to talk about the night before. But Ham said, 'Maybe he's really sick or something,' and we thought well, yeah, that could be. So he went in your tent to check on you, and then he came back out. And, ummm . . ."

"And . . . ?"

"Well. He didn't know what to do, he said. You were—you were passed out dead drunk naked in the middle of your bed, and he was ashamed and didn't know what to do, he said. So Japheth smacked him on the ear and said, 'So you cover him with a blanket and keep the embarrassment to yourself, blockhead.' But Ham just stood there like a moron. So Japheth and I got a blanket, and walked backward into the tent and draped it over you, and then went and did the day's work, and ate supper, and put the kids to bed, and everyone was just about asleep when I heard you moving around out here."

"By God I'll kill him," I said.

"Dad . . ."

The enemy drummers had increased their tempo again, and I drained my cup of water and poured myself another one and drained that one, too. And then I repeated it: "I will by God kill him."

"Dad. I know what he said and did was stupid, but he's probably more embarrassed by it than you are. So even though I know you're mad, maybe in the morning we can take care of this. Japheth and I will take him aside and try to teach him some better manners."

I was shouting by now. "Everyone up! Now! Everyone get out here!"

"Dad . . ."

"You shut up," I said to him. "I'll handle this."

In another minute we were all there. My three sons and their wives. All the grandchildren. My wife, who had wisely chosen to sleep in one of the other tents, rather than tolerate the mess I had made. She would clean it up, I knew, and never say a word about it; because all these years she has always been a better wife than I was a husband. All these years.

All these years, all these years, the drummers had joined in unison to hit that rhythm: all these years! All these years! Boom boom boom. All these years!

All these years, all the tears and struggles of a marriage, here I was coming off a drunk with a raging hangover, and I looked at her and knew she would always be more woman than I could ever deserve.

I looked around at the group. I looked at Ham. "You are such an embarrassment. You are such a blockhead," I said.

"Yes, father," he said, and hung his head.

"I am Noah," I declared. "I am tsaddiq, a man of righteousness, and in a world full of wickedness I have found favor with God. This earth has long since turned corrupt, full of violence in every way: and when God looked here and there across the face of the land seeking a righteous man, he found only me. And so the Lord chose me, because I was tsaddiq, a man of blameless integrity. I am Noah. I am the righteous one chosen by the Lord. And now I pronounce a curse, in God's name."

Everyone gasped. Ha! They knew I had the power to curse, and they were afraid now! The enemy drummers were not afraid, though, and up till now they had just been toying with me: now they meant business, and the pain was going to make my head split wide open in another minute. But I was full of rage and pain and shame, and it was all going to erupt in the most severe curse I could give. The last shreds of my integrity were trying to object: "Who is the real sinner here, the man who claims to be a tsaddiq who falls down naked drunk, or the simple-minded son who is baffled and doesn't know what to do about it?" But the shame and the pain and the rage had wrapped themselves into a whirlwind, and I could not let go.

I pointed at Ham. He closed his eyes, bit his lip: he knew it was coming. Then he opened his eyes again, and looked at me, and waited for his doom.

"Cursed..." Ham's wife started to sob.

"Be..." My finger pointing at Ham's heart was like a spear of rage. And then I turned just enough to point down toward the boy standing between Ham and his mother: "Canaan!"

"Cursed be Canaan," I said again. "His life shall be misery and servitude! He shall be the lowest of slaves to his brothers!" My voice had risen to a shriek as the curse poured forth: "From generation to generation I curse you and all your descendants: you are slaves forever!"

Even by moonlight the shock on the little boy's face was plain to see. Ham the ox stood there stunned, and his wife started to wail. I looked at my wife. She looked at the ground. I felt wretched. I was more stupid than Ham, more cursed than Canaan, caught on the spear of my own rage, and the fury of taking my hangover out on someone else had not made the shame go away but had increased it tenfold.

"Stop that weeping," I commanded. "Everyone go back to bed."

And as they moved to obey, I walked out into the wilderness under the light of the moon, sat down on a large rock, and began to talk to God.

"This is all your fault," I told God. I knew that this was not the most polite way to start a conversation with the Creator of heaven and earth; for all I knew he would choose to blot me out for my rudeness. If the enemy drummers didn't give up pretty soon, though, blotting me out would be a mercy; and whichever way it went, I didn't really care at this point. God had answered only with silence, however. So I said it again, just for good measure: "This is all your fault."

"Indeed," God replied.

"If you were looking for a wise and righteous man, a man of integrity, to preserve and bless his family, the family of a tsaddiq: well, you should have done a better job of finding a tsaddiq who actually had some wisdom, righteousness, and integrity."

"It's an interesting point," God conceded. "But you know, it's hard to get good help. Even if you're God, you often have to make do with what you've got to work with."

"I've just cursed a boy because his father felt all awkward and embarrassed and didn't know what to do about the fact that I was passed out drunk and naked in my tent. I've just condemned a child to slavery, him and the descendants that will spring from him, for all future generations. And why? Because I was ashamed of my own behavior, and dying with this damned hangover. And so rather than admit that I was a stupid drunken fool I wanted to take it all out on Ham, and so I cursed his son because I figured that would hurt him even worse than anything I could do to Ham himself."

"It appears to have worked," said God. "The boy and his mother have cried themselves to sleep, but Ham is lying there staring into the dark, with a hole in his heart as big as a camel, completely devastated by your curse and clueless about what he should do now."

"I am pretty clueless myself, at the moment," I said. "What should he do now?"

But this time God did not respond.

"What should he do now?" I asked again.

Still no answer came. Then I saw that I was asking the wrong question, and so I changed it: "What should I do now?"

"What do you wish to do?"

"Oh God, I don't know," I said. "I wish I could make it so that all of this mess would go away. I wish I could make that curse go away. I wish I could make my stupid anger and resentment go away so that I would never have had an occasion to speak that curse. I wish I could fix my own behavior of drinking till I was so wasted I lay there in a naked drunken stupor all day long: I wish I could make that go away. And oh God I wish I could make this hangover go away."

"I can take care of that last one, anyway," said God. And just like that, the hangover was gone. The enemy drummers had vanished. All that was left was quiet and calm. And memory. And guilt.

"You can't do that," I said. "You can't take away the hangover and leave the curse in place."

"Do you know, it's always so . . . interesting . . . when you humans make declarations about what I, the Lord God Almighty, am not able to accomplish."

"I didn't mean that you don't have the power to do it," I said. "I mean that it isn't right for you to do it. It's not right at all."

"Noah, you may be a tsaddiq, but according to your recent testimony the lack of righteousness in your own character leaves you not in a good position to be lecturing me about what counts as right. But be that as it may: are you telling me you want those drummers back? Because if you do, I can . . ."

"No!"

"Well, then, that hangover is now history. Count your blessings. And remember, the next hangover might be even worse."

I closed my eyes and did three rounds of my breathing exercise—slow inhale, hold; slow exhale, hold—repeat; repeat—and I marveled at breathing without the pain of those enemy drummers in my head.

"Thanks," I said.

"You're welcome."

"Now fix the curse."

No answer.

The sound of my voice, hanging in the air from my abrupt command, seemed harsh and wrong in my ears. So I tried again. "Please fix the curse."

Silence. Deep, deep silence. I thought I could hear the faint sound of starlight falling on the earth. But I could hear no word from God at all.

"Please fix the curse. It is my fault, not the boy's. He doesn't deserve to suffer for my sin."

"That's true. He doesn't deserve to suffer for your sin. 'Deserving' often has very little to do with 'suffering.' Certainly you have cursed Canaan to suffer in ways he does not deserve."

"Then you'll fix it?"

"No."

"But he doesn't deserve it!"

"Indeed."

"Then why won't you revoke the curse?"

"Why don't you revoke the curse yourself?"

"Ah," I said. I had not considered this. A curse was a powerful thing: once uttered, it was an established fact. Nobody could change it. Everybody knew that. But what if 'what everybody knew' was mistaken? What if I gathered everyone back together in the morning, and said, "I behaved very badly last night: like a stupid drunken fool who should have hung his own head in remorse before his family, instead of taking his anger out on others. I spoke words in my anger: painful words, bitter words: a terrible curse. I hereby revoke these words: I am ashamed of what I did, and ashamed of what I am that I should behave that way, and ashamed of my words. I revoke them. They have no more force. There is no curse on this child."

I saw that I could do that.

I did not know if they would believe me.

I did not know if I would believe me; because I did not know if it was true.

When you speak a word into existence, it takes on a life of its own. You make a promise, and people believe you, and you cannot simply go back later on and say, "You know, I didn't really mean that promise, so it has no force, and we'll all just be content in pretending I never said it."

Or someone asks if you have finished the work that was assigned to you, and you say Yes, thinking you will finish it soon enough, before anyone has the chance to find out that you weren't quite done at the moment you said you were. Then they see the work, still incomplete, and they remember that you had said it was all finished; and they conclude that they cannot believe you when you say things. After that has happened, you cannot successfully explain that you want to change your answer about whether or not your work is done. Nor can you successfully renegotiate the meaning of the word "Yes."

If I went back on what I had spoken, I would certainly be humiliated in front of them; and it would be very difficult to accept that role for myself. I was not sure I had the courage to do that. And maybe that wasn't even the most important point. The really critical issue might be this: I would have taught them that whenever I uttered a word, they would not be able to know that it was utterly true forever. For all they could tell, I might already be planning to revoke it the next day. Or I might mean it at the time, and then change my mind later on, and revoke it then.

I could see the problems that might cause. I did not like the image of people thinking I was a terrible cruel tyrant who might utter a harsh curse that was completely unfair. Still: didn't they have to know that whatever I said was absolute and irrevocable? Didn't they have to know that if I cursed you, you would stay cursed forever, because there was no way that that curse would ever go away?

"They all heard me speak the curse," I said.

"Indeed."

"Can you—can you turn back time? Can you call it a mistake, call it a 'do-over,' and start this sequence again so that I can get it right this time, so that it's like two days ago, and I have not started on my drunk, and none of this mess has taken place? You are God, after all; you can do anything, isn't that right? So could you make it so that nobody ever heard me speak the curse, because I never spoke it; because I didn't get angry; because I wasn't ashamed; because I didn't pass out in a drunken naked stupor?"

No answer.

"I mean, seriously, you do have the power to turn things back and make it so it never happened, isn't that right?"

No answer.

I said, "I am really sorry for this mess that I have made."

"I am quite familiar with that feeling."

That was surprising. How could God make a mess? How could God be sorry for making a mess? If you're God, don't things always have to come out the way you want them? All of these questions came crowding into my mind, clamoring for answers; yet I felt suddenly quite shy about whether I could ask those questions or not. So I said, rather hesitantly, "I don't understand."

"Let me tell you a story," said God. "Kind of a parable. So: let's suppose that once upon a time I gazed down from heaven, and I saw that the wickedness of all the people of the earth was great, no matter where I looked. There was no nation that did right, no family that did right, no individual that did right. I had been looking and looking for a tsaddiq, but I could not find one. I wished to bless those who were righteous, and so I searched for people of compassion, people of generosity, people who did what was right even when no one was looking, who acted justly even when they did not feel like it: even when it was against their own self-interest. But I could not find any. Not one. All across the face of the land, I could not find a single individual that I could genuinely identify as a righteous candidate for my blessings.

"And after a while it occurred to me that I was sorry that I had created all this: all these people, with such great potential for joy and goodness and fulfillment; I had given them life, and what had it come to? It grieved me to my heart.

"Let's say, then, that on some particularly aggrieved day I said, 'That's it, I've had it. I am going to blot it all out. I will wash the slate clean and start over; and since it is a very large slate it will take a lot of water to wash it. I will begin again as if none of this had ever happened; because I am sorry for this mess that I have made. All this so far has been a mistake, and so I am going to fix it; I am going to fix it with The Great Do-Over.' That's a very useful term, 'do-over,' by the way. Thank you."

"You're welcome," I replied. It seemed like the right thing to say. I felt nervous, though. God was driving at something, but I couldn't tell quite what it was.

"So let's see," said God. "How might the story go from here?"

I was not sure whether this was a rhetorical question or not. I waited. I thought if I didn't say anything, God would take up the narrative again. But the silence seemed to indicate that it was my turn, that God was waiting for me to say something. I pondered for a moment, and then

I shrugged. I did not know how to answer God's question, and so that's what I said: "I do not know, Lord. What would happen next?"

"The next thing that would happen would be this: I would see that the destruction I had in mind would make the violence of mere humans seem like nothing at all compared to the violence that I unleashed. A robber, a pirate, a warlord might be responsible for killing hundreds, even thousands; but I would kill hundreds of thousands, I would become the slayer of thousands of nations, I would sweep them all away: man, woman, and child. I would destroy the man whose heart was full of evil, and also the man who was mostly just trying to mind his own business; I would kill the child who had learned how to be cruel to animals and was learning how to be cruel to people, and also the helpless newborn at the breast. All of them! I would envision all this misery and destruction that I was poised to release, and I would not have second thoughts that moved me to hold back my wrath. No, I would pour it all out, and sweep them all away in my fury. I would blot out their lives from this earth, call it a mistake, and start over as if none of them had ever existed; because I was sorry for this mess that I had made.

"But let's say that instead of wiping out every single human soul, I decided to preserve one human family: your family. For no visible reason, I decided to pick you. It was not that you were truly a man of righteousness; as we both have reason to know, you are not too consistent at living up to the blamelessly-walking-with-God picture of what a tsaddiq should be. Perhaps you were the best of a very bad lot, in a world full of people where the inclinations of their hearts run again and again to corruption and self-serving. Or perhaps you were not the best at all, you were just another average sinner: but you happened to be the one I picked, and thus you found favor in my eyes.

"So then, instead of wiping out you and your family along with the rest of them, let's say I decided to tell you to build an enormous wooden box. Then you and your sons did the heavy labor of cutting broad wooden planks, fitting them together, and carefully sealing them with pitch. The result would not be shipshape at all, just a big rectangular box that would be blown about on the water. I'd tell you to gather up the animals: a male and female of each kind, because not only all the people but all the animals would be wiped out, too. And so it would come to pass that the only ones who would be preserved from my wrath would be you: Noah and his three sons and their families, and the animals two by two, inside The Do-Over Box."

I did not know what to say to this. Once again I could not tell for sure if God was waiting for me to answer or not. Even if God was expecting me to say something, once again I felt like I had nothing particularly wise to offer in response. The silence stretched on for a long time.

Finally I said, "I guess I'd feel like I ought to be grateful, for the chance to be the star of the show, and for being preserved when all the rest of the world got swept away. Still, I think it would be a very difficult turn of events. In particular, I don't think you would look good, if you did that. You would appear heartless and unjust, if you destroyed not only the cruelest of villains but also the youngest of babies. What would you say? Maybe, 'It was because even the infants were wicked and violent.' Or maybe, 'I was just so upset with the way things were going that I needed to wipe them all out in order to start over.' I guess I don't see how either of those could work."

Again there was silence for long moments. I asked, "Is this story hypothetical? It's a parable, right, not something that you are actually going to do?" But God did not answer.

I listened to the silence.

Then God said, "Here is an astonishing thing, Noah my tsaddiq, my tsaddiq who proves to be not so righteous as a righteous man ought to be: here is an astonishing bit of foreknowledge for you to ponder. The day will come when people will tell a story about you and your family and all the animals riding on the sea for many months in the Do-Over Box, and they will think that this story is cute."

I said, "I do not know this word 'cute.' What does it mean?"

God said, "It means sweet, or darling, or pretty."

"I do not understand," I said. "I know that I am not sweet, or darling, or pretty. At the moment I need some way to clean myself up from the stench of vomit and spilled wine and old sweat. And that's the easy part. Most of all, I need some way to clean myself up from the guilt of being a mean old drunk who humiliates a child to avoid humiliating himself. I don't think that could be considered cute."

"Indeed," said God.

"But why would anyone think the events in this story would be cute? Being blown around on the sea inside The Do-Over Box for months on end: that would not be sweet, or darling, or pretty. And the devastation of the flood itself, all those panicked people climbing trees and rooftops and struggling up to higher ground to try to be safe, and discovering that all their desperate efforts and prayers and hopes were in vain, because every one of them would drown in the ever-deepening waters: there would be nothing sweet, or darling, or pretty about that. Why would they call this cute?"

"Because they will find it easier to think of it as a cute little story to tell children, a story about happy animals two by two, so that they don't have to consider the devastation of all the world being swept away forever by the wrath of the Lord in The Great Do-Over. It is easier to call it cute and pretend that it is a cheery story, so that you do not need to explain 'what does it mean, if God is sorry for making this messy world, and decides to sweep it all away and start over?'"

"Are you sorry for making this messy world?"

"Sometimes."

I pondered this. What does it mean, I asked myself, if God is sometimes sorry for making this messy world? And then: what would it mean if God decided to sweep it all away and start over? As soon as I asked that, I could see one thing clearly enough. I could see that it would be possible to wash away all the sinners from the face of the earth; but as long as God put a few of them in The Do-Over Box to preserve them, that would solve nothing: there would still be the same problem with human sinfulness afterwards. You could never solve the problem of human sinfulness by destroying all the sinners except for Noah the tsaddiq and his family; because in the end you would still have to deal with me, Noah the drunk, and the messy consequences of my actions.

"Yes," said God. "You see it, don't you?"

I did see it. Or most of it, anyway. I saw that God had told me this parable about The Do-Over Box in order to let me see that this do-over strategy would not work for God: the consequences of certain actions are just irrevocably there, and if you try to wipe them out you end up wiping everything out, creating consequences that are far more devastating than the problems you already had.

I saw, also, that that meant that if the do-over strategy wasn't going to work for God, it clearly wasn't going to be the next thing that would happen for me, either. I had created a series of events, with my drunkenness and humiliation and rage and my unjust curse, and those events had now happened. God was not going to roll back time and give me a do-over on this; instead, the consequences of my actions were now real. I hated those consequences, but there they were, inescapably there.

I saw something else. I saw that even if God would not fix my problem the way I wanted, that didn't mean God would never do anything. In fact, it didn't mean that God would never be able to fix problems like mine in any way at all. I had felt like I was dying from my morning-after headache, and God had made my hangover go away; and perhaps one day it would come to pass that God would find a true tsaddiq, some man of righteousness whose wisdom and goodness would be far greater than mine, who would find the means to make my guilt go away.

But I could see one more thing, which would be true until such time as that. As for me, right now, I was stuck with the consequences of what my actions had created.

8

Sometimes It Causes Me to Tremble

> *Were you there when they crucified my Lord?*
> *Oh, sometimes it causes me to tremble . . .*

THE OTHER MEN WOULD tease Thutmose when he arrived at the mill in the morning, but Thutmose found he really didn't mind all that much. It was three weeks after his wedding, and every morning he arrived at work with a spring in his step and a silly lopsided grin that just never went away. Except once in a while, when he would start yawning and yawning and had to go splash some water on his face. He saw the winks the men gave each other. He half-heard the jokes they made not-quite-behind his back. But he just shrugged and grinned some more. His fellow workers shook their heads and laughed: they remembered what it was like, to be newly married and all full of the discovery of young love.

Then the annual rostering notice came. All young men, seventeen and eighteen years old, spent time in the army: it was his turn on the rotation. Thutmose would spend the next month in training. Most of it would be marching, many hours every day. It always was: that's what soldiers did the most. Beyond that, they would spend several hours each day practicing the fighting skills of infantrymen.

So, early in the morning on the first of March, he showed up at the barracks. About half the soldiers were second year boys, age 18; the remainder were first year soldiers, 17 years old, like Thutmose had been last year. They were assigned to regiments and squadrons, and got their equipment: weapons, packs, blankets. By late afternoon they headed out into the desert, two hours of marching before they made camp for the night.

The first three weeks passed with a steady routine. They had marched many miles. Thutmose had thought he had been in pretty good shape from his hard work at the mill, but almost day by day now he could see the toughness growing in his muscles. Through the bright mornings and burning afternoons the sun beat down on the soldiers in his division, as they ran and exercised and skirmished. At night in camp they would eat their rations, and then roll into their blankets, falling asleep almost instantly. And Thutmose would dream of his lovely young wife. It was no surprise, how his heart shivered when he considered her beauty: such has been the case of young husbands with their wives since time began. Yet she seemed to be enraptured by his beauty as well, with her eyes flaring as she looked at him, and her fingers trembling when she ran her hands along his muscles. So Thutmose was looking forward to her reaction when he got home, with his new sleekness and strength.

Four days before the end of his month on duty, the captain called them together. Apparently a large group of slaves had escaped from the capital. Several units of the standing army were in pursuit of the runaways: but their own two divisions of reserves, already out in the desert on their annual training rotation, had also been detailed to help round up those slaves. So they would be marching hard the next two days, to get ahead of these fugitives. The captain said he had no information on how well armed these runaways would be, but the men needed to assume that these would be hostile enemies. The intention was to capture them, rather than kill them, because slaves had much more value as slaves than as corpses: but if it came to a fight, the fugitives would not be "just practicing." When they fought, they would not be careful to avoid hurting anyone. They don't have your training or equipment, the captain said. But they can still kill you dead. Look sharp, people.

Thutmose thought about that. He'd had a month of training a year ago; now he had had almost another month of playing soldier: add it up, and he was still far from being a professional army man. Even so, he thought the men in his division looked strong, ready for action. In the back of his mind he could hear a voice insisting that it had always been drill and practice before; this time, real people could die. Well, so be it. He took a deep breath. He thought he was probably as ready as he could be.

The next day was the longest, hardest-driving march Thutmose had ever experienced. The officers had them on the move in the dark, an hour before dawn. The column took one rest shortly before noon for the cooks to make hot meals, and another stop late in the afternoon for cold rations; and they finally made camp with just the faint traces of sunset still showing on the western horizon. The following day began the same way. Thutmose thought his legs were too sore even to stand up; but somehow the officers managed to shout and prod and kick everyone into line in the column, and they were off again. Weary and footsore, they were moving, back in the familiar rhythm of the march.

Late in the afternoon they came over the crest of a ridge and saw the sea. It was the most bizarre thing Thutmose had ever seen: it looked like a road leading down into a chasm in the sea. To the left and the right the sea was there, like mighty cliffs but made of water, and a canyon between them running from the shore down into the depths. There were people there: the runaway slaves. It looked like thousands of them, marching down between those cliffs of water. And off in the distance to his left Thutmose could see dust trails rising into the sky, indicating the approach of other army units: the horses and chariots of the professional army.

The general ordered them forward. Their two divisions of infantry were marching in from the southwest: there was a division of cavalry and a division of chariot archers, moving in from the west and northwest. Together the divisions of the army drew closer to those fugitive slaves, who were fleeing down that valley into the sea.

The head of Thutmose's column was less than two miles from the stragglers at the tail of the line of runaways. Everyone felt bone-weary from the last two days of very hard marching: but the adrenaline was in, with the rush of the army toward the prey. The prey were rushing too, with the adrenaline of feeling their enemy closing on their heels. The captain had them jogging along, a steady double-time pace, relentlessly eating up the distance as they drove down into the darkness of the sea, across rocks and sand and silt, with immense walls of water held in place by some impossible force. Thutmose thought about sticking his hand into that water. He was not sure if it was safe—what if he broke whatever magic spell was holding back the water—yet he couldn't quite resist reaching out his hand, as he jogged along. It really was water. He tasted it: salty: it was the sea. Huge crushing depths, on either side of them. High above he could see the sky, late afternoon blue: but it was dark, down in the bottom where he was. If those walls of water broke loose from whatever force had stacked them up—Thutmose wrenched his thoughts away from that, and concentrated on keeping his feet moving. He felt the burning in his legs and lungs: they were going uphill now, they had run across the bottom of the sea, they were heading up toward "normal" land once more.

He looked up ahead. They were gaining on the runaways, visibly gaining almost every minute now. The gap of two miles had closed to several hundred paces. As the road through the sea continued to climb it got lighter. Thutmose could see hills and trees in the distance up ahead, lit by sunset colors. Another few minutes and they would catch the runaways, about the time they all got to the beach.

Louder than thunder the water fell. Daylight was so close, but it was too far: the seas crashed around them, slamming men in every direction. Thutmose was stunned by the concussion. His weapons dropped from his hands, his eyes and mouth were full of muddy water, he could not see, he could not breathe, he could not tell which way was up. He could feel consciousness slipping away from him, as he tugged on his pack straps to drop the weight from his back: if he could only release that weight, he could make it to the surface, it had to be close, just one breath of air was all he needed. Then he saw his wife: the beautiful face of his wife, she was reaching out her hand to him. He spoke her name, he stretched to take her hand, longing to touch her hand one last time. But he could not.

On the beach, all our aunts and uncles collapsed in the sand, gasping for breath after their long desperate run. They were alive! They were alive, and God had destroyed their enemies.

And they began to gloat.

Perhaps they did not mean to gloat. In the wonder of discovering that you are still alive when you feared you were about to be horribly dead, you may not intend to gloat: you may intend just to wonder, and praise God, and offer profound thanks.

Yet sometimes it's hard to do that, without gloating.

Our family had been preserved, and set free. Uncle Moses broke forth into song: "God has thrown the horse and rider into the sea! God has taken Pharoah's chariots and drowned them in the deep waters. I will offer praise to my God, for he is a mighty warrior, and he has destroyed the men of Pharoah's army."

Perhaps it was right and fair and just, for our aunts and uncles in those long-ago days to hold a grudge against Pharoah—or at least, that particular Pharoah. Certainly the more recent Pharoahs had not been kind to them; indeed these Pharoahs had failed to provide justice for our family, preferring to offer them only two harsh alternatives: death, or eternal slavery throughout all generations. And so perhaps justice would genuinely allow our ancient aunts and uncles to gloat over the latest Pharoah's destruction.

Yet if it was Pharoah who enslaved them, Pharoah who gave the orders for the army to recapture or kill them, it was not Pharoah who was destroyed.

Was it right for our aunts and uncles to gloat over young men like Thutmose, their lives shattered in the falling waters? Was it good and fair to gloat over Thutmose's widow: a happy young bride, scarcely out of her honeymoon and now bereaved? Consider the Passover itself; what of all the first-born sons of the Egyptians who were struck down, what of all the bereaved young families, so full of joy at the birth of their babies, their life reduced to ashes as the angel of death struck down their children: was it justice, to celebrate the misery of these families?

Listen to me, my nieces, my nephews. Not all the stories within our family's heritage are happy stories. We must remember and retell these stories, and we must not gloss over the fact that our own behavior was not pretty. It has come to pass far too often within our family heritage that we have been rebellious, and we felt proud in our rebelliousness, when we should instead have repented in sorrow. It has come to pass far too often within our family heritage that we have arrogantly assumed we knew, when we should instead have been humble and teachable. And it has come to pass far too often within our family heritage that we have gloated, when we should instead have wept: when we should have wept with gratitude, and also wept with compassion.

It is not as if we have not felt the anguish, when we have been on the receiving end of hatred and taunting. When others have rejoiced because our feet have stumbled, we have cried to God, "Do not let them gloat over me." In the time of Uncle Micah, a time of deep distress, we knew that we must for a time bear the wrath of God because we had allowed our hearts and our behavior to drift far from the Covenant that God had made with us, then Uncle Micah found courage to declare on our behalf, "Do not gloat over me, O my enemy; even though I fall, I shall rise, and the Lord will give me light even when I sit in darkness." And remember how Uncle Obadiah scolded the cousins descended from Uncle Red: "You should not have gloated over us when disaster overtook us!"

And yet Uncle Obadiah engaged in a fair bit of rejoicing-over-somebody-else's-misfortune himself, didn't he, when he saw how bad the destruction would be for Uncle Red's family. Our family has indeed sung songs of praise at the thought of our enemies being broken with a rod of iron, dashed to pieces like a potter's vessel.

This is part of our story. We have been gloaters. I will not deny it.

Yet neither will I be proud of it.

The best I can do is to acknowledge it, in humility and repentance.

Listen well, my children. The heart of our family's heritage is not misery and destruction for those who hate us. The truest and best thing we have learned is not that God loves us, and hates our enemies. No: our God has revealed to us a mighty purpose for the redemption of all the world. Even at the best of times it is not obvious how such a plan could come to fulfillment for such a world as ours; and whenever one portion of that world is bent on destroying another portion, it seems impossible that the redemption of all things could ever come true. I have no doubt that if the enemy army had caught up with us, there at the sea, they would have been quite happy to gloat over our corpses; yet when we gloated over their corpses, we simply showed we could be just as good at hating as anyone else.

It is right, of course, for us to offer our heart-felt gratitude to God for sparing us from the destruction that nearly overtook us. It is right that we should sing songs of praise, songs of wonder and worship to our Lord, who had preserved our lives when we were so afraid that we were about to die. But the gloating reveals that we had not yet grasped that God's plan to deliver us from evil is not to deliver "us" by destroying "them," but rather to include us—all of us, even those who have been enemies—in the redemption of all things.

Perhaps I can say, in defense of our family as we gasped and gloated there on the beach, that no one had yet taught us that.

It remains true that we had not managed to see it on our own.

So when we had caught our breath, we stumbled to our feet once again. Uncle Moses began to sing, and we rejoiced in the destruction of our enemies. Aunt Miriam got out her tambourine, and she began to dance: and all the women joined in, dancing in gladness there.

Then we marched into the desert.

There is food and water in the desert, if you know where to look for it; but there is only enough for a few people at a time. There could never be enough to feed the great multitude of us who had escaped. We had brought food with us, of course, but the amount people could carry was limited, and even that amount was reduced as some people dropped their burdens in the final desperate dash for the shore. If we had had only the food we carried or found, we would certainly have starved to death—and indeed some of us grumbled that Uncle Moses had brought us out of slavery just so that we could die of hunger in the desert.

But God brought down bread from heaven for us, so that we did not shrivel up and die. It was a tricky thing, this bread from God. We called it manna: a word that means, "What is this stuff?" At first light each morning, we would go out to gather it up: tiny flakes of food, strange stuff, you could boil it into a porridge or bake it into sweet wafers. God gave us each day our daily bread: always just enough for each family. If you decided to put some aside, just because you wanted to be prudent, just because you wanted to make sure you would have some tomorrow: why, then it would spoil overnight.

Yet on the sixth day—always and only on the sixth day—everyone would discover that they had gathered twice as much as they actually needed. No one meant to gather twice as much, and yet twice as much was what each family ended up with. When that happened, on this sixth day, the extra would not spoil; instead, it would be food for each family on the seventh day. Day by day, week by week, we marched through the desert; but we did not move out on the seventh day. We rested. We rested, and we ate the extra that was left over from the sixth day, for it had not spoiled overnight.

It took us several weeks to make it to the mountain. There, at the top of the mountain, God gave Uncle Moses the Covenant. There are commandments in the Covenant, of course, and people sometimes call it "the Ten Commandments" —as if the Covenant were only about obedience, and as if there were only ten specific things that we needed to remember to do. But you already know that the Covenant is more than that. It is fine to call it "the Ten Commandments" for short, if you like (although it is perhaps worth pointing out that saying "the Ten Commandments" is not actually shorter than saying "the Covenant").

Notice something, my children. It is something you already know, though you may not have specifically thought about it: the Covenant does not begin with commandments. It begins with story: a story about us, and about our relationship with our Lord. It tells it so briefly: "I am the Lord your God, who brought you out from the land of Egypt, out of the house of slavery." That summary of our story is the bedrock of our family's identity. This story tells us who we are. This story, briefly declared as the opening words of the Covenant, insists that we are people whose story begins with God: we are not the first to act or speak in this drama, because the one who has taken the action, the one who speaks and tells the story, is the Lord our God. We are the "you" as the story begins the Covenant, and so these words show us that we are the people who are addressed by God: "I am the Lord your God, who brought *you* out from the land of Egypt, out of the house of slavery." The story reminds us that we are the people who had ended up in slavery in a foreign land, helpless to free ourselves: but God acted to set us free. That's who we are. The one-line story included at the beginning of the Covenant obviously does not include things that happened earlier or later in our family history, and it doesn't fill in any details beyond this single sentence. Yet it identifies who we are as a people, who we are as a family, with just this brief summary of how God told our foundational story: "I am the Lord your God, who brought you out from the land of Egypt, out of the house of slavery."

Then comes the part of the Covenant that everyone remembers, with ten commandments about loyalty, Sabbath, inviolable relationships, and desire. You have all memorized that part—or certainly should have by now, if you have been studying your lessons—so you will not need for me to repeat that for you.

But I do want to tell you the very next thing that happened. The Lord gave the Covenant to Uncle Moses: and here is what happened, right after that.

We had all seen what God could do. Bringing us out of Egypt, marching across the bottom of the sea, arriving safe on the other side. Providing food and water for us, as we made our way through the desert to the mountain. Seeing things like that, we all knew that God is mighty. Yet when we saw these things, we were only seeing the results of what God had done. When we got to the mountain, we saw more. We saw brilliance like lightning at the top of the mountain, in the midst of wreaths of smoke; we heard the sound of trumpets, and thunder that seemed to shake the very earth itself, and certainly made all of us tremble to the depths of our souls. These things that we were seeing at that time, they were not simply the magnificent results that remained after God had acted: they were the indications of the very presence of the Lord our God, and we were so afraid. Shivering with awe and fear, we drew back. We called out to Uncle Moses, "You speak to us the words of God, and we will listen; but don't let God speak to us, or we will die."

And then Uncle Moses said just the strangest thing.

"You do not need to be afraid," he said. "God has come to test you, so that the fear of the Lord will be in you, to keep you from sin."

So it was that Uncle Moses told us that we did not need to fear; we only needed to fear. God did not want us to be afraid, said Uncle Moses; he simply wanted us to be afraid. Ah! Wouldn't it have been a fascinating thing to be there when he said that, listening to the hubbub among our people at that moment! "What does that mean?" they must have asked one another. "What does it mean, if Uncle Moses tells us that God doesn't want us to fear, he just wants us to fear?"

Or perhaps not. Perhaps there was no hubbub. Perhaps they saw it clearly; just as perhaps you have already seen it, my nieces and nephews. Perhaps you already have the wisdom to know that words don't always mean one and only one thing. Perhaps you already have the wisdom to know that "to fear death and pain and suffering" is one thing, but "to fear the Lord" is quite another thing. Both of them are shivery feelings, of course; both of them include the awareness that we are not quite in safe normal everyday circumstances. Perhaps the best word we have for this is "tremble."

Remember, my children, how our hearts were trembling, remember how our souls felt like they were going to burst with fear, in that mad panicked scramble up the last hundred paces to the shore, with the Egyptian army so close at our heels. We were filled with fear, fear of our enemies and fear of the pain that they were about to inflict upon us. Remember when the waters fell, and we were still alive at the very moment that we thought we were going to feel the sharp weapons of our enemies slashing into us, pouring out our life's blood upon the sand: and our hearts trembled with astonishment at what God had done. Remember those few moments, before we began to gloat. In those moments of awe, of astonishment and gratitude and wonder: then our souls trembled with the fear of the Lord.

That's what Uncle Moses declared to us, there at the mountain: God does not want you to tremble (in the terror of those who reckon they are about to be tortured and killed); instead, God wants you to tremble (in the astonishing awe that the Lord Almighty loves you, and makes this Covenant with you). Perhaps they saw it, right at that moment. They did not need to be afraid, with sick dread at how the glory of this awesome God might simply burn them away into nothingness, there where they stood. Instead, their hearts could tremble with worship and adoration before the Lord who radiated such splendor.

9

Days When the Lord Didn't Tell the Truth

> *Therefore God said he would destroy them—but Moses, his chosen one, stood in the breach before him, to turn away his wrath from destroying them.*
>
> —Psalm 106:23

"IT'S NOT MY FAULT!" said Uncle Aaron, and maybe that was right. Certainly he had a very difficult and frustrating task, and insufficient instruction, and way more responsibility than he was expecting. It is arguable, at least, that there was enough blame to go around.

Uncle Moses had disappeared, and that was very worrisome. Everyone depended on Uncle Moses. Certainly his brother Uncle Aaron did. But Uncle Moses had headed up the mountain. Uncle Moses had decided to take with him only Uncle Joshua, who was just a young man at the time; he had told everyone else to wait there at the bottom of the mountain; and then the two of them had climbed up out of sight. They had not come back.

Uncle Moses was supposed to meet with God up at the top of the mountain: but how long was that supposed to take? It had been days. People tried to be patient, but day followed day, two weeks, three weeks. Had Uncle Moses and Uncle Joshua fallen off a cliff? Or been eaten by wild animals? Should we organize a search party to look for them? Should we just keep on waiting? No one knew what to do.

Uncle Moses had been to the mountain previously, before he had come to lead us out of Egypt; and then when we got to the mountain, Uncle Moses had gone up the mountain, taking Uncle Aaron and Uncle Hur and seventy elders with him. That's when God had spoken to him the words of The Covenant. But this time he had only taken Uncle Joshua. Uncle Joshua had not come back to tell of any accident that had happened. Had both of them been killed? Or was everything fine?

"Are we supposed to just stand around, camped out here in the middle of the desert, until our food runs out and we all starve? Where's this 'land of milk and honey' supposed to be, anyway? If it's a long walk from here, let's get going." That's what people were saying.

Uncle Aaron was trying to be diplomatic. "Look, these things take time. We know we're supposed to wait for Moses, so we just need to calm down, and I'm sure everything will be fine."

More days went by. Four weeks. Five. The family had gotten very restless. "OK, so we are supposed to follow this God—the God of our ancestors. Well then: make us an image of this God. Something strong and virile, like a yearling bull calf."

"I don't think we're supposed to do that," said Uncle Aaron. He was pretty sure that when Uncle Moses had spoken the words of The Covenant, there was something in there that forbade the making of images.

But the people were insistent. Uncle Aaron felt trapped. The whole family, twelve great tribes, clans without number, were looking to him for guidance, and he didn't know what to do. Maybe his brother Moses was indeed dead. It was almost six weeks since he left. Had he taken any provisions with him? Maybe Uncle Joshua had something in his backpack, but Uncle Aaron was pretty sure Uncle Moses had had nothing in his hands, and no sack on his back. Obviously he intended to be back in at most a day or two, and though there was still smoke and thunder on the top of the mountain, there had been no sign of his brother in all that time.

So one of the clan leaders spread a big blanket on the ground. Everyone started tossing donations of various kinds onto that blanket: earrings and pendants, even large bracelets of solid gold. It became quite a substantial heap of jewelry. Uncle Aaron didn't know what to do. If his brother was dead, the leadership of all these people would fall to him: he had to lead them somewhere, in the name of God, and he didn't know where that was, or what God wanted.

Several members of our family, skilled potters, made a great crucible out of clay, while others gathered wood and built a fire. We set the crucible in the midst of the fire, and banked up the coals all around the crucible, while the potters formed a mold out of clay as well. Uncle Aaron felt like he was in a trance, sleepwalking through the process. We all felt pretty much the same: it seemed as if the gold found its way into the crucible, all by itself: and then poured itself into the mold all by itself as well. When the gold had set, we turned it out of the mold onto the ground, and several of the craftsmen set to work finishing the idol, shaping, shaving, shoving it back into the fire to burnish it, then pulling it back out and working it some more. All night long we labored on it, and in the warmth of the early morning sun the calf seemed alive with inner fire. All the family bowed down before its radiance, offering our worship to the strong and powerful God who had brought us out of Egypt.

Meanwhile, up on the mountain, God had now given The Covenant to us in writing.

The finger of God had written the words of The Covenant on two tablets of stone for us. Ah, what would that have been like, to see the finger of God etching letters into a slab of granite! Then God had started giving Uncle Moses additional laws, laws to cover a variety of situations. God had just finished giving him instructions on how to build the sanctuary. It would be a mobile sanctuary, which we could take down and carry from place to place, as we were travelling through the wilderness, and then set back up again when we arrived at the next encampment. There were instructions about curtains and lampstands, utensils and vestments.

God then reiterated to Uncle Moses the importance of the Sabbath as a perpetual sign of The Covenant, which all of our people were to keep through all generations. Then God said, "Except—there aren't going to be any more generations. The people have turned aside from my commandment, and made themselves an idol. My wrath is burning against them. I will consume them all. I will start over again with you, and make your descendants into a great nation."

Moses fell on his face before God, and implored him, "Do not do this, O Lord! These are the people you have brought out of the land of Egypt by your great power—do not give the Egyptians the chance to scoff, 'Their God took them out into the wilderness, but only in order to kill them!' Turn away from your fierce anger, and remember your promises to Abraham, Isaac, and Israel. Change your mind, O Lord, and do not bring disaster on your people." And God agreed not to destroy us.

Notice this, children. God had declared, "This is what I'm going to do!" Uncle Moses, a mere human, made his plea, and then the Almighty One decided not to wipe us out after all. The word of God was delivered, but not fulfilled.

Uncle Moses scrambled to his feet, and headed back down the mountain as quickly as he could. Even though Uncle Joshua was a young man in his prime, he had to hustle pretty hard to keep up with Uncle Moses, already an old man, as he strode down the pathway from the summit.

As Uncle Moses and Uncle Joshua came around the last curve in the path down the mountain, they saw it all: the calf, the people bowing down, and Uncle Moses' own brother up front. Uncle Moses was . . . not pleased.

He had the tablets of the law in his hands. God had spoken the words of The Covenant to Uncle Moses, and he in turn had declared them to all of our people, and we had all responded in great fervor, "All that the Lord has commanded us, we will do!" Then Uncle Moses and Uncle Joshua had gone back up the mountain, and there the Lord had cut two stone slabs from the sheer rock face of the mountain, and engraved the words of The Covenant onto those two tablets of stone. These two pages-carved-in-stone would be the everlasting declaration of The Covenant that our God had made with us.

But as he saw all of our people worshiping the golden calf, Uncle Moses hurled the two stone tablets against a boulder. They shattered into a thousand fragments, symbolizing that the law of God had been utterly broken even before Uncle Moses had the chance to show the family how the hand of God established The Covenant with us in tablets of stone.

"You shall have no other gods besides me," it says in The Covenant; and "you shall make no representations of anything, in heaven or on earth, and you shall not bow down to them." We had heard this word when Uncle Moses stated The Covenant for us. Yet we had really only heard it that one time, and it went against generations of experience in a world where making an image to represent the Divine was a common occurrence. The day would come when we had recited the words of The Covenant from generation to generation many thousands of times, memorizing it so well that it was not merely learned by rote, but learned by heart, with a knowledge that had become part of our very souls: but that day was not yet. It was all so new to us, in those days. We had not yet seen the words of The Covenant that had been inscribed in stone by the hand of God. We were such beginners, at keeping The Covenant.

That did not stop Uncle Moses from being mad. "What are you *doing*!?" he screamed at Uncle Aaron.

"It's not my fault!" he replied. "The people were desperate with uncertainty. You were gone so long, we thought you were dead. They wanted to worship. They wanted to see God in a form they could follow. So they gathered up a pile of earrings, and I just . . . threw the gold in the fire, and out came this calf. What could I do?"

The "I didn't do it, it did it itself" excuse has never worked all that well; certainly it didn't work well for Uncle Aaron, in that moment. Uncle Moses was angry, and that was a fearsome thing to behold. He called out: "Who is on the Lord's side? Come to me!" All the descendants of Uncle Levi came running. "Take your swords," said Uncle Moses, "and work your way across the camp and back again, and strike people down. Even if it is someone you know, your neighbor, even your brother, strike them and kill them." And that's what the Levites did. Three thousand of our people died there.

Yet Uncle Aaron did not die. Many died that day, being struck down by this word of judgment: but Uncle Aaron was not among them. Uncle Moses had given the severe command, to slash people at random, even your own brother, so that they would fall bleeding into the desert sand and die: but Uncle Moses did not slash his own brother, and no one else slashed Uncle Aaron either.

We moved on from there, grieving, wondering, penitent, perplexed. We wanted to be faithful; we wanted to do what is right, moment by moment and day by day. Yet we were still such beginners at following The Covenant. Often it seemed we were much better at whining about it than at obeying it.

Then it came to pass, after many more months of traveling through the wilderness, God again got very angry at us. This time it was because of all our complaining. God had gotten upset at us quite a few times along the way, for our hardness of heart, our slowness to believe. But on this occasion it was even worse. The wrath of God poured forth once again in a furious declaration that we were all going to be destroyed.

Here's how it happened.

God, Uncle Moses and all the rest of us were deep in the desert. We had left our life of slavery behind us, and we were heading for the

Promised Land, the land flowing with milk and honey, the land of abundance and freedom and goodness. But it was a long walk. It was hot and dusty every day. We were not walking in a straight line. Everyone had sand everywhere: in all our clothing, in all our food, in our noses and in our ears: everywhere. It was all pretty miserable, and when people have the miseries, they do tend to talk about them.

It's not like we really wanted to complain—nobody had said, "When I grow up, I want to be a world-class whiner"—but the fact of the matter was that there was serious moaning and groaning going on in the ranks. We were all tired, and we wondered if we were ever going to get to this Promised Land, and people were even beginning to think fondly of our life back in Egypt.

We had been eating manna from heaven for many days. It was good, full of strength and nourishment, but it was boring. People hungered for real food: meat and vegetables, varieties of taste and texture. We had animals with us, of course, and we could slaughter them: but people were quite hesitant to start doing that. Those animals represented our future. They would be our flocks and herds on our farms, in days to come. We could slaughter them and feast now: but then what would we do, when we got to the Promised Land, and there were no animals left to build new herds with? So we ate the manna, and complained.

"If only we had meat to eat," people said. "Remember the fresh fish we used to eat, in Egypt? And the melons! And all the vegetables: cucumbers and onions, all spiced up with cumin and dill and garlic!"

It got Uncle Moses pretty upset, and he expressed his frustration to God. Not that God necessarily needed the information—"Excuse me, Lord, I'd just like to bring to your attention a few facts that you might not have known about"—but Uncle Moses needed to tell someone, and God was close at hand to listen.

"You didn't do me any favors, Lord," said Uncle Moses, "when you put me in charge of all this crew and made me responsible for them. It's like all they can do is grumble and complain all day long! I'm so tired of hearing all this whining."

"Tell me about it," said God.

"Well, they talk like they are nostalgic for being slaves, and they whine that they don't have any fresh meat, and . . ." Uncle Moses paused, and then gave a nervous laugh. "Oh. You didn't mean for me to fill in all the details, you were just commiserating."

God said, "Let me tell you what I'm going to do. First, we'll appoint seventy elders, and put them in charge of listening to most of the whining. And then I'm going to give them meat. Ha! It won't be enough for a big day-long feast: it won't be enough for two or three days: it will be enough to last a whole month, till it runs out their noses and they hate it."

"That's a lot of meat," said Uncle Moses. "Are you sure you can find that much around here? It's pretty dry and barren in this region."

"Do you think my powers are limited? Just watch and see whether I can make my word come true or not."

Then the Lord inhaled, and the sound was like the deepest sigh in the history of all time. Then God blew: and you might expect that it would be like a hurricane, but it was not: it was not furious in its force, but it was godly in its reach, for this gentle wind stretched out to touch all the earth. And the breath of God gathered up quails: millions of quails. Not pheasants or chickens, not starlings or wrens or owls, but quails. All around the camp the quails landed on the ground. Miles in every direction they were stacked up on top of each other. Quails everywhere, piled up, waist deep. All the people went out to gather them; we just picked them up, wrung their necks, and put them in sacks. We roasted some of the meat and dried the rest.

Yet some of us died with the meat in our mouths, struck down by a plague sent by God to punish us for our whining. Our God can be quite severe, at times. We have not always learned obedience easily.

In due course we came to the edge of the Promised Land, the Land of Milk and Honey, the place of rest that God had promised to us, the place we had been heading all this time. Uncle Moses appointed twelve spies, one from each tribe, to go in and check the place out. All of the rest of us waited impatiently for the report.

When the spies returned, they came back with two reports instead of one: a majority report and a minority report. All of them agreed that it was a rich land, indeed it was a land flowing with milk and honey, just as we had been told. They even brought back an immense cluster of grapes, so full and long and heavy that they had to thread a thick wooden rod through it so that two men could support it on their shoulders as they made their way back to the encampment.

Ten of the spies spoke up and said, "The land is good, but the people who live there are like giants, compared to us. They looked at us as if we were mere grasshoppers, and that's how we felt, too, when we looked at them."

But the remaining two spies, Uncle Joshua and Uncle Caleb, gave their report a little differently. They said, "The land is rich and the people there are indeed big and tough. But God will be with us. This is the land that our God has promised to give us, and so we will conquer it, and thus we shall live in the blessing."

All the people listened to these two reports. We thought about the richness of the land. We looked at that amazing cluster of grapes, so big and full and heavy it took two men to carry it. And we thought about the giants in the land, and our hearts quailed in fear. We said, "Perhaps it would be better to look elsewhere; perhaps some place where the current occupants might be a little . . . smaller . . ."

God did not like it when we responded this way. God had been mad when we made the golden calf, and three thousand people were slain. God had been mad when we complained about the manna and whined that we wanted meat, and many more died. It is a fearsome thing, when the wrath of God breaks out in judgment against us.

And on this occasion, God got so mad that once again this very odd thing happened. God said something that turned out not to be true.

I know some of you are hesitant to believe me, when I tell you that God said something that turned out not to be true, but that's how it was.

God said to Uncle Moses, "That's it. I have had it up to here with these people. I am going to wipe them all out, every man, woman, and child, and start over. I will make a great nation from you, Moses, and will fulfill my purpose with you and your descendants, instead of this rabble of rebels who complain and grumble endlessly."

That's what God said. It was just like before, when we had made the golden calf. On that previous occasion and now again on this one, the will of the Lord had been revealed directly to Uncle Moses. It was quite clear. Yet notice this, children: notice this. Notice what Uncle Moses did not say in reply. Uncle Moses did not say, "May God's will be done." Uncle Moses did not say, "If this is the way God wants to do it, then this is how it is going to happen." Uncle Moses did not say, "The proper response, the faithful response, when the intention of the Lord has been revealed, is to accept it in humility and obedience." Any of those statements would have been an authentic expression of what Uncle Moses actually believed. Yet he did not say any of them. He said something quite different: "God, this is the wrong plan you have spelled out here, and I am here to tell you that you should change your mind."

Now think on this, my children. Think on this, both from God's perspective and from the viewpoint of our people, down through all the generations. Is it possible for God to change his mind? Whether you pick Yes or No as your answer, it seems problematic. If we say Yes—and many of your aunts and uncles have said Yes, over the generations—then it seems that God does not necessarily pick the best plan to start. If, as many have supposed, any change would have to be change for the better or change for the worse, then a God who changes would either have started or ended with something less than the best. How is such a thing possible?

On the other hand, if we say No—and many of your aunts and uncles have said No, over the generations—then we face the problem that what God told Uncle Moses was not what God was planning to do. He told Uncle Moses that he was going to wipe out the entire family, knowing that Moses would object, and that God would then "appear" to change his mind and forgive us, while really doing what he had planned to do all along.

That solves the problem of God changing his mind, but the cost is quite high: because we have ended up with the conclusion that God deliberately said something false, in order to trigger a reaction from Uncle Moses.

Which is worse, a God who says what he truly intends to do and then sometimes changes his mind and does something else, or a God who sometimes declares that he is going to do something that he has no intention of fulfilling, in order to trigger a particular reaction from the person listening? Wait, what's the word for someone who does that, anyway? What's the word for someone who deliberately says something that isn't true? Isn't that the sort of person we call a liar?

Is it better to accept that God sometimes changes his mind, or to accept that God sometimes lies?

It is pretty awkward, whichever way you answer. Whichever solution we choose, however, we still have to deal with the fact that what we have heard God say, what we have even written down as the Word of God, might not be the final and absolute truth. For God said, clearly and distinctly, that he was going to wipe out all our family. Yet what God had said turned out not to be the truth: for God did not wipe out the family.

This reality teaches us something important: if we only consider part of the story, and then assume we know what God intends (because that's what that part of the story seems to have told us, quite plainly), our assumption might well turn out to be mistaken, because we haven't heard the whole story.

This situation ought to press us toward humility—which is a place we rarely want to go—a humility that refuses to claim to know more than we actually know. We must not take any single line, divorced from its context, near or far, and consider it as a statement of absolute truth. Yet if we were to make this uncertainty a principle in its own right, we would never believe anything at all.

If we needed to have absolute certainty before we could do anything, then we would just be permanently stuck, because we've just seen that we don't necessarily have that kind of certainty: what God said might be subject to change (or, if you prefer, what God said might be deliberately deceptive in order to elicit a certain response from someone).

Humility, then, comes in recognizing that we are always limited in what we say. Our comprehension is not complete. We do not deal in certainties, but can only offer up the best understanding we have so far.

Our best understanding can indeed be quite persuasive; we can have quite a bit of clarity about quite a number of things. Yet even at our best, it is only our best so far; and we may discover along the way that we have been quite mistaken about something we thought we knew. Even when the thing we thought we knew came straight from the mouth of God.

This does not need to be a reason for distress. Indeed, the only reason for it to be distressing would be if we were planning on using the words we read in the text as a weapon. If our goal were to prove that we were right and our opponents were wrong, then it would be quite handy to be able to quote a line and then conclude that we have absolute certainty on our side, and therefore our opponents must be wrong. Because we generally derive pleasure from an earnest debate—and especially if we win—it's nice to have an unbeatable trump card we can play over and over again, whenever we need it: ha! I have a scripture text! I win!

Yet consider this. Even if we knew that any and every line that has been written in the Bible could be chosen at random and then stand alone as an absolute truth—we have seen that this is not the case, but let us suppose for a moment that things were this way—even then, this would only work as long as all of us never read those lines, never quoted them, never used them. Of course you can see why this is. We certainly could not claim that we ourselves, mere readers, mere quoters, mere fallible people who made an application from text to life: we could never claim that *we* will do *our* work flawlessly. Even if we knew that the words from God's own mouth could never be subject to change, we could never have absolute assurance that we won't hear them wrong, understand them wrong, or apply them wrong.

These two occasions when Moses argued against God's decision were not the only time this sort of thing happened, you know. Something similar took place about six centuries later, in the time of Uncle Amos. Those were hard times for our family. We had managed to split into two rival factions. In the north we called ourselves Israel, and we included most of the territories: Reuben, Simeon, Issachar, Zebulun, Dan, Naphtali, Gad, Asher, Manasseh, and Ephraim. In the south we were just two territories, Judah and Benjamin, and Benjamin's population and territory were relatively small and so the southern kingdom was usually just called Judah.

We had been one unified nation, under the leadership of King Saul, and then King David and his son King Solomon; but when your Uncle Solomon's son, Uncle Rehoboam, became king, he managed to alienate people pretty severely with his policies, and we ended up with the northern kingdom (Israel) and the Southern Kingdom (Judah). By the time Uncle Amos came along, almost two centuries had passed since that division, and we had had more-or-less constant border disputes and other squabbles between the two kingdoms.

There was a problem, though, when Uncle Amos began his work as a prophet. If I tell you that Uncle Amos was from the south, but God called him and sent him to talk to the people up north, you can see where some of that problem came from. God had sent Uncle Amos from his home in the southern kingdom of Judah to rebuke the members of the family in the northern kingdom of Israel: and when he rebuked us for being so stubborn in our resistance to the things God had called us to do, we didn't want to listen to anything this fellow from down south had to say.

You can see how it would go, when the farm boy from down south showed up to tell all the sophisticated northern folks that we weren't getting it right. All the stubbornness kicked into high gear. One afternoon one of our chief leaders from the northern kingdom, Uncle Amaziah, spoke quite bluntly to Uncle Amos: he told him to shut up and go home.

That was quite ironic, considering that earlier that morning Uncle Amos had been doing his daily devotions, and in those devotions God showed him a vision. Sometimes people get a sense of what God is up to through reading the ancient words of scripture. Other times individuals find out what God has in mind through words that they "hear" well enough to state: "Thus says the Lord." But Uncle Amos was a little different from either of these: he found out what God was about to do by seeing it in a vision: a vision where God showed him beforehand the punishment God had decided on for us.

It was a vision of locusts. Uncle Amos saw that God had decided to send a terrible army of locusts who would eat up everything: the grass in the field, the grain in the barn, the vegetables in the garden, the clothes on the line, the bread on the table. It was a vision so vivid that Uncle Amos didn't have to think about what it would mean. He saw it. He saw children naked and starving. He saw the corpses of emaciated families, dead in the dust, whole clans wiped out, nothing left but misery and dust. He saw it: saw it so clearly, as a fact that God had established. It must have been bad, for Uncle Moses, when he heard God say, "Thus says the Lord, 'I will destroy them.'" But what must it have been like for Uncle Amos, to actually *see* all that destruction, before it actually took place?

It broke Uncle Amos's heart, and he cried out to God in a great lament: "O Lord, relent, I beg you! Change your mind, and do not bring this disaster upon your people!"

And God responded to Uncle Amos's plea, saying, "This will not happen."

God showed Uncle Amos how something different would happen, instead, giving him a different vision. Instead of locusts, God would send fire. Fire is terrible and destructive, but it is quick. Instead of dying from the painful and slow judgment of starvation, our people would die from the painful and fast judgment of fire.

That might not seem like much of an improvement to you, and it didn't to Uncle Amos, either. His heart wailed: "Oh, no, Lord! Do not do this, I entreat you!" And God repented of this plan as well, talked out of fulfilling his intention by the intercession of Uncle Amos.

It is useless to plead that we shouldn't really count this either as a lie or as changing his mind, since God hadn't actually *said* it to Uncle Amos; he had only *shown* it to him. God may have chosen one method or another to communicate the message, but whether in writing, or in spoken words, or in a visionary demonstration, God had communicated to Uncle Amos what he was about to do.

Uncle Amos, deeply pious, constant in his devotion, willing to leave his home in obedience to God, persevering in going to people who didn't want to hear what he had to say: he did not respond to these two visions by saying, "If this is what God has decided, then this is what will be. I am your servant, O Lord." Uncle Amos did not say, "Thy will be done on earth, as it is in heaven." Instead, his heart cried out for God to do something different from the plan that had been revealed to him. And God hearkened to the plea of Uncle Amos. The decision of God changed. The will of the Lord was revealed: and then a different, changed will of the Lord was revealed.

Sometimes the change is very rapid. Remember Uncle Hosea? About fifty years before the time of Uncle Amos? He heard the voice of God, and knew that he would have to declare what he heard to our people: "I made you my children, I taught you to walk, I led you with such compassion and love"—that's the message God gave Uncle Hosea to deliver. "Yet you have kept sacrificing to the Baals. You keep offering worship to idols. Well, I have had it. You will be slaves to the Egyptians once more, and to the Assyrians, too. Warfare will rage against your cities. The sword will strike down your people, because of all your schemes. Since you are bent on turning away from me, I am not going to rescue you when you get around to calling on the Most High."

Pretty grim words. Sometimes I wonder how Uncle Hosea must have felt, as he heard God declare such a severe judgment. I suppose Uncle Hosea might have stopped listening then, filled with despair for all our family, for surely it is correct that we have been stubborn and willful and have forgotten and ignored the word of our God. Perhaps Uncle Hosea might have stopped listening, so overwhelmed by what he had heard: this authoritative declaration of judgment and destruction. From God's own mouth this word had come, and now it was for Uncle Hosea to write it down: a devastating word of destruction. Perhaps Uncle Hosea might have stopped listening, and with tears on his face and deep sorrow in his heart he took up parchment and pen and wrote them down, so that this heartbreaking word of the Lord might be established and preserved forever as the truth that God had declared, and which many would then assume could never be contradicted or altered.

As it turns out, though, Uncle Hosea did not stop listening, and so he learned that this word of the Lord could indeed be contradicted and altered, because God changed his mind and contradicted what he himself had just declared. The enemies of Uncle Daniel made much of the fact that the law of the Medes and Persians cannot be revoked: how much more, then, would we suppose that the word of God could never be revoked. Yet that supposition would be mistaken, because God Almighty chose to revoke it. And because Uncle Hosea had not stopped listening, he heard the word of God that contradicted God's own previous statements: the declaration of the severe judgment on our people, of our reaping destruction as the well-deserved punishment for all our many sins, would turn out not to be the truth after all. For what God said next to Uncle Hosea was this: "How can I give you up, my children? How can I hand you over, O Israel? My heart recoils at the thought of your destruction; my compassion grows warm and tender. I will not execute my fierce anger: for I am God and not man, I am the Holy One in your midst, and I will not come to destroy."

Do you remember, children, when King Barak of Moab hired the prophet Balaam to curse our people? (No? Some time soon I will need to tell you that story, too.) On that occasion, in one of his oracles Balaam declared, "God is not man, that he should change his mind." Yet Uncle Hosea heard God using the very same God-is-not-man argument in the exact opposite direction: namely, to indicate that God was perfectly capable of changing his mind. Human parents might well become so frustrated with a rebellious child that they come to the point of saying, "That's enough, I've had it, you are banished from my house forever." Yet when our God feels those same feelings, it doesn't mean we will get the same results we would get if you or I were that frustrated with relentlessly disobedient children. God is God-and-not-man, and thereby has both more capacity for truth than we mere humans do (and so Balaam the prophet was correct when he said that), and also more capacity for compassion than we mere humans do (and so Uncle Hosea was correct when he said that).

And there is more. There are a couple of times when this same thing happened with Messiah Jesus as well. The first was near the start of his public ministry, when he and his followers and his mother, Aunt Mary, were all invited to a wedding. During the reception the groom's family ran out of wine, and Aunt Mary pointed this out to her son—with the same tone of voice that mothers always have used to indicate to their children that they are expected to take care of the situation. When your mother tells you, "Your room needs cleaning" or "There sure are a lot of dirty dishes," she is not simply giving you information: she expects you to take action, to do something to fix the situation. You would not be well advised to take her words as if they were nothing more than a statement of fact; it would not be wise for you to respond by saying, "I admire your powers of observation, Mother. Truly you have a keen eye." So when Aunt Mary said, "They have run out of wine" to her son, he heard the implied instruction that she expected him to take care of the situation. With some exasperation, he let her know that he would not take care of it, because it was not the right time for him to act. Yet even though his answer indicated that he would not do it, she simply turned to the servants nearby and told them to do whatever Jesus instructed them to do. He then did what his mother had requested: he had the servants fill some clay water storage jars with water, which he then turned into wine and saved the reception. Messiah Jesus had been asked for a miracle and he had indicated that he would not do it; and then she persuaded him to change his mind, so that the first thing he said turned out not to be the final truth.

On another occasion Messiah Jesus was traveling with his followers well north of Galilee, and a local woman—some say her name might have been Justa—saw him and recognized him. She immediately came and pleaded with him, asking him to heal her daughter (her name, some say, was Bernice). Messiah Jesus said that he would not perform this healing. Moreover, he indicated that his mission was to the lost sheep of the house of Israel; indeed he offered a proverb with rather a harsh edge to it: "it is not right to take the children's bread and throw it to the dogs."

You or I might have found such a refusal too daunting. It certainly would not be surprising if Justa had gone home in tears, to care for her daughter Bernice for a few more days until the girl died. But Aunt Justa did not give up so easily. She matched Messiah Jesus proverb for proverb, responding that even the dogs under the table get to eat the scraps that the children drop. When Messiah Jesus heard this, he must have laughed with delight: for he changed his mind, and although his response to Justa had indicated he would not heal Bernice, in the end he did heal her. And so the first answer he gave turned out not to be the final truth.

Have I shaken your faith, children? I hope not. But I hope that I have indeed challenged your faith. I hope I have challenged your faith to understand that just because it is written, that does not mean that it is the final word. I hope I have challenged your faith to have the courage of Uncle Moses, of Uncle Amos and Uncle Hosea, of Aunt Mary and Aunt Justa: so that when you hear a word of judgment or denial from our Lord you may have the courage to say, "No, Lord. You are a God of compassion and mercy, and I entreat you to change your mind, and forgive and redeem and heal your people in their need." I hope as well that I have challenged your faith toward humility, toward the recognition that even when you are very sure you know exactly what a word from our God means, you can have the patience to recognize you may not have heard the very last word on the subject.

And perhaps I may say, in my own defense, that I am not the one who first told these stories. They are far older than I am. I merely pass them along. I pass them along because they are stories that we need to know, for they are the stories that tell us something important about who we are: we are the people who believe that even when we have heard a word from God of destruction, refusal, or hopelessness, that might not be our Lord's last word on the subject. We are the people who remember that when God spoke to Uncle Moses and declared that for our sins we would all be destroyed, Uncle Moses said, "No: change your mind, O God"—and God did. We are the people who remember that the word of condemnation God had declared did not come to pass: for God is God-and-not-man, and did not come to destroy us.

10

Prophet for Hire

As we traveled through the wilderness, from campsite to campsite, we began to get a reputation among the nations around the edges of the wilderness. "There are fierce people, living in the desert," they would say. "They march for days across the burning sands, and their god provides water and food for them. No army can stand before them, because their god fights for them."

They told these tales to frighten children into behaving well: "if you are not good, the wild desert people will come and get you!" That made the young children cry, and gave them bad dreams; but perhaps it also motivated them to try to be good—at least for a little while.

The point of wandering through the desert was not to gain a fierce reputation, of course. It was not to teach the children of other nations to be good. It was to teach *us* to be good: to teach us to rely on God. Alas, we did not learn this lesson easily.

Among those who were frightened by our reputation was Balak son of Zippor, king of Moab. It may have given him bad dreams, but it didn't make him cry, because he was a king and needed to find a solution, rather than just feel sorry for himself.

His advisors told him, "They fight in the name of their god, Yahweh. Perhaps, indeed, Yahweh fights for them. Perhaps that is why they win all their battles: no one is able to withstand the wrath of Yahweh."

The situation seemed pretty hopeless to King Balak. How could a little nation like Moab withstand the wrath of Yahweh? Probably not even a great nation like Nineveh or Babylon could survive, he thought, against the wrath of Yahweh. If one of the gods decides to wipe you out, then that's what happens, you are just gone, and soon forgotten.

Yet as he pondered on this, King Balak considered that the gods were notoriously unreliable, and often capricious; sometimes they could be persuaded to take a hand in human affairs, but you never knew for sure. Suppose the Israelites could be deprived of the help of their god; suppose Yahweh could be persuaded to stop supporting them? Wait, what about this: suppose Yahweh could be convinced not only to stop fighting on their behalf, but instead to work against them? Suppose instead of blessing them, Yahweh could be persuaded to curse them?

So King Balak asked his advisors, "Who do you know who is good at divination? I need someone who could offer an offering to the god of the Israelites, one that would be more pleasing than the offerings they themselves offer. We need someone who would know how to talk to Yahweh better than they do. If you know of some prophet like that, perhaps we can hire him to split the attention of Yahweh away from these people, or even to curse them in his name, so that he no longer fights on their behalf."

One of his advisors said, "May the king live forever! I have heard of such a prophet. His name is Balaam son of Beor. He lives a great distance to the east, in the city of Pethor on the Euphrates River. It is said that he can prophesy in the name of twenty different gods. Whether it is true or not I do not know; but if it is true, this might be the man that my Lord King Balak seeks."

So Balak son of Zippor, king of Moab, sent four royal messengers to the east, to the city of Pethor on the Euphrates, to hire this great prophet, Balaam son of Beor. They brought with them a substantial fee to pay for the divination. They traveled many days on the caravan route until they came to the Euphrates River, and then followed the river to the city of Pethor, and found the house of Balaam son of Beor. They presented themselves before him, and humbly laid the divination fee on the ground before him as well. And they presented the words of Balak son of Zippor, king of Moab: "Come to me, mighty prophet, and curse my enemies for me. They are a wild desert people, fierce and dangerous; they have come to the borders of my land, and we fear that they will defeat us, for they are more numerous than we are. What is more, they have a god, Yahweh, who has blessed them and who fights on their behalf. But I have heard of your great reputation: whoever you bless is indeed blessed, and whoever you curse is indeed cursed. So come, curse these people for me, in the name of their god, Yahweh."

It was certainly an interesting offer. Yet Balaam son of Beor knew better than to pick up this option without examining it carefully first. "You must wait a day," he said to the messengers of King Balak. "I will inquire of this god, Yahweh, and see what I can learn of this matter."

That night Yahweh appeared to Balaam in a dream. Notice this, my nieces and nephews. This is an astonishing thing, is it not? Our God appeared to a man who was an outsider to our people, in response to a request to curse our people. The message God gave him was to instruct Balaam that he was not to go to the land of Moab with King Balak's messengers. "You shall not curse the people these men want you to curse, for I have chosen to bless them."

Thus it was that in the morning Balaam spoke to the four officers from the court of Balak son of Beor, king of Moab: "Return to your own land. I cannot go with you. Yahweh has spoken to me, forbidding me to accompany you." So the four of them returned to King Balak, and gave him the unwelcome news that Balaam had refused to come and curse King Balak's enemies.

King Balak considered this. He did not know for sure what Balaam's standard fee might be; he wondered whether the money he had offered him might have been low, perhaps even insultingly low, thus causing Balaam to react, "What? You think you can hire me with the same fee you would pay for someone to come and pray for rain for your crops?"

Or was this refusal perhaps one of Balaam's standard negotiating ploys; the man might not be insulted, but he still wanted more money for the job than Balak's first offer.

So King Balak again sent messengers to Balaam son of Beor, in the city of Pethor on the Euphrates. This time he sent eight of them, all of them nobles: they were high advisors and princes, carefully instructed to show great honor to Balaam the prophet. The eight royal officials gave this message to Balaam: "Again I entreat you, mighty prophet, to come to Moab. Do not think that I regard you as unimportant, for I intend to do you great honor when you arrive. Do not think that the offering my messengers set before you last time was the entire fee I will pay: that was just intended as a down payment on the riches I will bestow upon you once you have come here and cursed my enemies."

Balaam replied to the eight messengers of King Balak, "Suppose your king were to give me enough silver and gold to fill his house. Even then, I still could only say whatever Yahweh told me to say. Being a prophet means I can let you know what God wants you to do. It doesn't mean I can make God do what you want him to do."

These eight advisors conferred among themselves, and then they said, "Look, we'll be in real trouble with our boss if we return empty-handed; so can you at least inquire of the god and see? Maybe he has changed his mind, from last time. How much could it hurt to ask?"

Balaam had no quick rejoinder for that, so he told the messengers to wait for a day, and he would inquire. That night God appeared again to Balaam, and said, "You shall indeed go with these men who have come to summon you: but you shall only do or say what I command you." So in the morning Balaam arose, saddled his donkey, and went with the officials of Moab.

It was a journey of many days. They travelled in a small caravan, with four of King Balak's officers out in front, scouting for bandits that might be lying in ambush; then Balaam and his two servants; and then the remaining four officers serving as the rear-guard. At night, around the fire, the nobles from King Balak's court filled in more of the background about the kingdom of Moab, and about these wild desert people. They spoke of the wealth that King Balak intended to give to Balaam, and the honor and acclaim that the king intended to shower upon him— all for cursing these wild desert people, in the name of their god.

Balaam remembered the word of Yahweh, that he was only to say whatever Yahweh told him to say; but perhaps he did not remember that quite as well as he remembered all the talk about the wealth and fame that he would receive in payment for the simple job of cursing King Balak's enemies. A simple job: travel to Moab, curse these people, collect his fee, and carry the money back home.

Perhaps that is why the anger of God was kindled against Balaam. The command of Yahweh had been plain enough—say exactly what I tell you to say—but perhaps mere words were too easily forgotten, when men were speaking of great riches around the campfire each evening. Perhaps that is why God decided to bring the lesson home to Balaam, at the point of a sword.

The following afternoon an angel of Yahweh appeared suddenly in the road. Balaam was riding on his donkey, Hepzibah, nearly dozing in the early afternoon heat. The four officers in the vanguard had passed a point in the road, and they had seen nothing, because nothing was there: but then the angel of Yahweh was there, still as a statue, with a drawn sword pointing right at Balaam. Balaam saw nothing. But the donkey saw, and she skittered off the road and into the field, to avoid the danger in the road: the angel of death standing there with sword extended.

Balaam nearly fell from the saddle when Hepzibah had jumped off the road like that. He looked again at the road, and saw nothing there: no reason for her to have turned suddenly off the road to avoid something. He whacked the back of her head with his fist, and then hauled around on the bridle to bring her back onto to the road, muttering under his breath about what a stupid animal she was.

An hour later they began to pass through a region of vineyards. Some of the vineyards were on open hillsides, set back from the road; but some of the vineyards came right up to the edge of the road, and they were protected with stone walls, to keep the road traffic out of the vineyard. There was a place where the road narrowed as it passed between two walled vineyards. The four nobles in front rode through without incident, but as soon as the last of them passed the angel of Yahweh blocked the road again, with sword pointed straight at Balaam's heart: death waiting motionless as a rock. Balaam saw nothing. But once again Hepzibah the donkey saw, and she shied away. There was not much room; as she skipped to the right Balaam's right foot and ankle got scraped between the donkey's girth and the stone wall. The angel of Yahweh slowly pivoted, the sword tracking toward Balaam: and so the donkey cantered rapidly past, scraping and banging his foot against a dozen rocks in the wall.

Balaam swore, whacked at Hepzibah again, and yanked at the bridle as he pulled her back onto the road. Blood was oozing out of four or five painful scrapes on his lower calf and ankle. He looked at the road behind, trying to see if there was a snake or something that made the donkey jump off the road like that. Balaam's servants had stopped, and the officers in the rear guard had stopped, but they had seen nothing in the road: they had just seen that the donkey had shied off the road for no apparent reason. Balaam saw the puzzled look on their faces; he saw the questioning way they glanced at each other. What's with this guy, that he can't keep his donkey on the road, that he gets his leg all torn up? That's what they seemed to be thinking.

Balaam smacked Hepzibah a couple more times for good measure. "Stupid beast," he muttered. "Stupid, stupid beast."

The road went on, and the little caravan followed it: four nobles from the court of Balak son of Zippor, king of Moab, riding now two by two; then Balaam son of Beor, the prophet, with bloody scrapes on his right calf and ankle, along with two servants; then the remaining four officers. The road wound its way into the rugged hill country, and soon was climbing toward a pass between two peaks. Ahead of them they saw where a rockfall had brought an immense boulder down the mountain, narrowing the road as it passed between the face of the cliff, on the left, and the boulder on the right. The four officials at the head of the line rode through this gap, single file. As the last one passed between the cliff and the boulder, suddenly the angel of Yahweh appeared yet again, drawn sword pointed at Balaam. There was no way to pass on either side. The donkey stopped. Balaam kicked her hard, urging her forward. But Hepzibah saw that she could not move forward. He kicked harder: and she knelt down right there in the road. Balaam was so angry. He beat on the donkey with his staff.

At that moment, God took an unusual action, and the donkey's braying became speech: "Why are you beating on me like this!" Whether the miracle was in Hepzibah's mouth or Balaam's ears, I cannot say; but in either case the donkey spoke and the man understood. Yet though he understood the words, he did not yet understand their real significance. He did not yet understand that there was more meaning here than just the meaning of the sentence the donkey spoke.

I do not know that you or I would have grasped this revelation any more clearly; for when our hearts are aflame with anger we never do our best work. So often we get so riled up that we merely react to the words someone speaks, without considering what other significance these words might bear: and when that happens, we sometimes miss moments of great import.

That's what was happening for Balaam, in this moment. Hepzibah his donkey had spoken a discernible sentence. That's not something donkeys ordinarily do. At such a moment a person might well pause and ask, "What kind of miracle might this be? What might be going on, if God has suddenly altered the normal course of events so that an animal can speak words that a man can understand?"

But Balaam was not ready to ask such a question, for the anger was in him. Hepzibah had asked, "Why are you beating me like this," and all Balaam could do was blurt out in self-justification: "It's your own fault!

You have made a fool of me before these men. Why, if I had a sword in my hand, I'd kill you right now!"

Hepzibah said, "And yet I am your donkey. You have ridden me for many years. Have I been in the habit of behaving this way?"

Balaam said, "No." He didn't say anything more than that, out loud: but in his soul he did say more. He thought, "That's right. Hepzibah never behaves like this. Her shying off the road *means something*. Something very unusual." Then Balaam realized, with a sudden shock, that the most unusual thing wasn't that Hepzibah had jumped off the road, but that she was conversing: asking questions, and indeed making Balaam work to answer those questions. Something astonishing was happening: what might this mean?

What it might mean became clear a moment later, when Yahweh opened Balaam's eyes to see the angel, standing in the midst of the narrow pass between the cliff and the fallen boulder, with the sword pointing directly at him. The angel was still a dozen paces away, and yet it felt somehow as if the point of that sword was almost touching the bridge of his nose. Balaam stared for half a moment, feeling nothing but panic: and then he rolled off the donkey's back, fell to his knees, and then prostrated himself on the ground.

The angel said, "That's an excellent question, don't you think, that the donkey asked? Why have you been beating her? I have stood on the road as your adversary three times now, ready to strike you down with this sword. Mighty prophet that you are, you didn't notice anything amiss: yet each time your donkey has had the wit to recognize the danger of walking blindly into the wrath of Yahweh. Because she had the wisdom to fear the Lord, I would have let her live; but as for you . . ."

Balaam answered, "I have sinned." Nobody really likes feeling like a sinner, and especially nobody likes to admit to being a sinner out loud: but even though it is awkward, it is most often the cleanest thing you can do. "I have sinned," said Balaam, "for I did not know that you were standing on the road to oppose me. If my journey is displeasing to you, I will turn back, at your command."

The angel of Yahweh said, "Go on with these men to Moab: but you shall surely remember to say only what I tell you to say." Balaam nodded. Then the angel was gone. Balaam got up from the ground and got back in the saddle, and he and the officers of Balak rode on.

As for those officers, what did they see and hear? Were their eyes opened as well, so that they saw the angel with the drawn sword? Or did they see that Balaam's donkey had stopped, and then knelt on the road, and then brayed while Balaam talked to her: and then Balaam had suddenly slid from the saddle and had laid himself facedown on the ground, while talking to some unseen being? Did they figure out that the visionary must be having a vision? Or did they themselves also see the object of Balaam's vision, the angel of Yahweh standing with drawn sword? No information about this has come down to us. Whichever way it was, those court officials certainly saw that something was happening: the great prophet Balaam was on his knees and then flat on his face in obeisance to something or someone far beyond their ordinary human experience.

At least, that's what happened for the four officers who were in the rear guard of the caravan. The four who had ridden in advance saw nothing. They had gone through the top of the pass single file and down the other side for a few minutes before they realized that Balaam had not followed them through the pass. They reined in, and waited for another minute or two, and still no one came through the pass. Feeling anxious, they turned around and rode back; but by the time they arrived it was all over, Balaam was mounted on his donkey and heading into the pass.

Around the campfire in the evenings they compared notes with each other, and asked Balaam what he had seen and what he had heard. Perhaps he told them everything; perhaps he gave them an abbreviated version. However much he said, they could tell that the experience had crystallized a renewed sense of obedience within the prophet, for the angel of Yahweh was not to be trifled with. No conversation about wealth could overcome the certainty of that vision of the angel with the drawn sword. Balaam was very clear in his own mind: he would speak only what Yahweh gave him to speak. That had become very clear to the officers as well, and when they made their report to King Balak, they would need to make sure the king understood what had happened, and what that meant.

A hundred generations later it would come to pass that many a preacher would take comfort from this story, thinking "If the word of Yahweh can come forth from the mouth of an ass, then there's hope for me." Yet that would be far in the future; and as the caravan approached the border of Moab, two of the officers hurried on ahead, to make their report to King Balak. The king received their report, with its word of caution; but he was delighted that their embassy had succeeded in bringing Balaam the prophet to the land of Moab. He went forth in person to greet Balaam at the border, and to welcome him into the land.

"I'm so glad you have come," he said. "I am ready to show you great honor, and to reward you richly for setting a curse on these wild desert people, in the name of their god."

Balaam nodded his head in acknowledgement of Balak's words, as he strove to be clear in his response: "I have indeed come, O King, at your invitation. Yet let me say again, I cannot speak just any word, at whim. Whatever word God puts in my mouth, that and only that is what I must utter."

King Balak heard this, but he did not take it too seriously. "This is the sort of thing prophets always say," he told himself. "But in the end this prophet has come here to curse these people for me, and so of course that's what he will do." So King Balak ordered a great sacrifice of sheep and oxen, in honor of the gods of Moab, and he ordered that a substantial portion of the lamb and beef be roasted and set before Balaam as a great feast of welcome.

The next morning King Balak took Balaam into the hill country of Bameth, to a high valley. From that spot they could see out into the wilderness, and they could see a portion of the encampments of our people. In his soul King Balak was nearly dancing with excitement, but his words were calm as he pointed toward our people and said, "Behold, these are the wild desert people, whom I brought you here to curse."

Balaam did not respond to the implied instruction that he should go ahead and curse them right now. Instead, he asked that seven altars be prepared, and that seven bulls and seven rams be slaughtered, a bull and a ram for each altar, along with plenty of dry wood. When the stones of each altar had been assembled, the dry wood was carefully arranged on top of them: a nest of very fine tinder at one end, ready to flare up hot at the first touch of flame; overlaid by a large pile of kindling, but with room between the kindling pieces for the fire to breath; and then crisscrossed with larger pieces of wood, to burn high and hot for an hour or two. Then eight men, straining hard, had lifted the whole carcass of the bull up on top of that thick layer of wood. They placed the dead ram on the altar as well, beside the ox. A man with a burning torch stood beside each altar, and when Balaam nodded his head, each torchbearer thrust his torch into the nest of tinder and kindling. Seven altars blazed as the fire rapidly spread to all the dried wood, and the aroma of smoke and roasting meat filled the valley.

Balaam looked around the valley, and chose a bare hilltop overlooking the spot where they were standing. He said to King Balak, "Wait here, beside your burnt offerings, while I climb up over there." He pointed to the high ground and said, "Perhaps Yahweh will come and meet with me, up on the crest of that hill. Whatever he shows me, I will report to you."

So Balaam hiked across to the hill he had pointed out, and then made his way to the top. There were no trees or grass or even dirt there: just a bare slab of rock. Balaam the prophet knelt there, waiting to see if Yahweh might meet with him, or speak to him.

He had waited for several minutes in silence. It was awkward. He knew that King Balak and his court officials were too far away to see him well, but they were still close enough that they could tell the difference between a man who was standing and a man who was kneeling. Certainly they were expecting him to do something. But Balaam had nothing to do but wait. So he waited. Nothing happened. He waited. He wondered how long he might have to wait. He was not sure how long his knees would stand it, if he had to keep kneeling here for an hour or two or three. How long would he stay here kneeling, before he gave up and returned to King Balak to say, "Sorry, Yahweh apparently is not interested in meeting with me today."

Yet as it turns out, Yahweh actually was interested, for suddenly Balaam was aware that the presence of God was all around him. Almost without conscious thought his posture changed, from kneeling to lying face down on the ground before the presence of Yahweh. "May my offering be acceptable in your sight, O Yahweh," he said. "I have arranged for seven altars, each with a bull and a ram for a burnt offering, to be a pleasing sacrifice for you."

And our God spoke to Balaam. "I shall give you the word that you must speak. When you return to Balak, this is what you must say to him."

Then Balaam son of Beor climbed back down from the hill and made his way back to the place where King Balak and his officers were waiting. They had been sitting on the ground, watching from afar. There had not been much to see, though, so mostly they had been talking. One of them had fallen asleep. At one point someone had noticed that the prophet was no longer kneeling, but was lying face down on the ground: they commented on that for a moment. No one could see anyone but the prophet up on top of the bare hill: was he taking a nap up there, or was he talking to an invisible god? They could not tell.

When they saw Balaam climb back to his feet and start climbing down from the hill toward them once again, they had guessed he must have had a vision, for he would not be returning so soon if he had nothing to say. So as Balaam arrived at the place of sacrifice, with the seven altars, King Balak and his men were all on their feet, looking attentive and respectful.

Then Balaam lifted up his voice and began to sing: "Balak has brought me from Aram. The King of Moab called me from my home in the eastern mountains. 'Come, curse these people for me,' he said; 'come, denounce this nation Israel, these wild desert people.' Yet how can I curse those whom God has not cursed? How can I denounce them, if Yahweh has not denounced them? For I have seen them from the high hill, and my eyes behold them still from here: they are a people who live alone, and do not reckon themselves as one nation among many others. And they are many, more than the dust of the ground; they swarm, more numerous than the dust in a fierce dust storm. If I live a long and righteous life, I will still be looking at these people beloved of Yahweh and thinking, 'I want to be like them!' "

As far as poetry goes, it wasn't much. It wasn't even all that much of a blessing. Still, it wasn't any kind of a curse at all, and King Balak felt the balance tipping in the wrong direction. "What are you *doing*!" he hissed at Balaam. "I hired you to come here and curse these enemies of mine, to split them away from the blessing of their god, and instead of cursing them you have added a blessing to them!"

One of the things that a person needs to recognize about conversing with God is this: you have to be clear about which one of you is God, and which one isn't. You may be quite certain what it is that you are trying to get God to do, but in the end you really don't have a lot of leverage with which you can force God to do your will. Balaam had seen this, but Balak had not yet grasped this lesson. So Balaam said, "I'm just trying to tell you, as carefully as I can, the words that Yahweh has put in my mouth." He sounded kind of pompous, in his own ears, when he said it; but he had said what he had said, and there it was.

King Balak was not ready to give up. "OK, let's try this again," he said. He brought Balaam around to another place, farther south to the region of Mount Pisgah, where there was again a good view of the wilderness and the encampments of our people. "Look at these people: as numerous as dust, as you say. As numerous as lice or locusts, I would say instead, and as bad. Curse them for me, as you look on them from here. Curse them in the name of their god, and then they will truly be cursed."

Balaam gave them directions again, to build seven altars with seven burnt offerings, with a sacrificed bull and ram on each altar. Once again Balaam went aside, up to a high place, and waited to see how Yahweh might respond. Then God spoke to him; and he returned to King Balak, and this is what he said:

"Stand up, Balak, and hear this oracle: listen well, son of Zippor. There is a difference between God and mortals: God does not lie, or change his mind, like humans do. He has promised, and he will do it; he has spoken, and will fulfill it.

"I have received from God a command to bless, for he has blessed, and I cannot revoke this blessing.

"As for these people you want to curse, God Almighty decrees no misfortune for them; he foresees for them no trouble. Yahweh their God is in their midst, and they acclaim him as their king forever. Their God has brought them forth out of Egypt, and he fights for them with the power of a wild ox, with the ferocity of a lion. There is no enchantment or divination you can use against them; in the end it will be said, 'See what God has done on their behalf!'"

This was not what King Balak wished to hear. He wanted to interrupt the words of the prophecy. He wanted to command his men to strike down Balaam in mid-sentence. But sick dread had fallen upon him, and when he had heard this oracle all he could say was, "Do not curse them at all, and do not bless them at all." It was the closest he could come, at that moment, to telling Balaam to just shut up.

King Balak considered this situation for two days, and then he decided to give the project one more try. It might be, as Balaam had declared, that the god of his enemies did not lie or change his mind; but a decree of blessing could surely be revoked, if the god who gave it decided he wanted to do something different. And that was the point, wasn't it: to find the words or the offering that might persuade this god that he wanted to do something different.

Thus King Balak said to Balaam, "Come now, I wish to show you these people from a different place, where you can see many of their encampments, and see what a menace they are. Perhaps it will please their god that you may curse them for me from that vantage point." So they journeyed to Mount Peor, and from there they could look out into the wilderness and see our people, spread out in their encampments tribe by tribe.

Once more Balaam instructed the officers of King Balak to build seven altars and prepare a bull and a ram for each altar. The sacrifices were made and the burnt offerings were set ablaze. In that moment Balaam realized that he did not need to go aside and wait to see what Yahweh might say. The truth of what Yahweh was doing was clear to him. He looked out from the height of Mount Peor at our people, in their encampments, and it was clear that Yahweh had chosen to bless these people. There was no need for Balaam to wait for a sign in order to perceive what was happening. He just needed to take a good look.

He felt the Spirit of Yahweh prompting him, in that moment, and he opened up his mouth and let the words flow forth:

"Here is the oracle of Balaam son of Beor. It is the oracle of a man whose eyes are clear. It is the oracle of a man who hears the words of God, and sees the vision of the Almighty One.

"I sing in praise of the people of Israel: how fair are your tents, your encampments are like a great and lovely city. You are like vast orchards of palm trees, or like a well-watered cedar forest! You are like a series of gardens, stretching along a river as far as the eye can see, or like aloes planted by God Almighty in the largest farm ever.

"Truly this nation shall not lack for water or for sustenance, and its kings and their kingdom shall be highly exalted. Their God brings them forth out of Egypt, and he fights for them: he will crush anyone who opposes them, and devour the nations who make themselves his foes. Sooner poke a sleeping lion than rouse the wrath of Yahweh! These people are blessed, and those who bless them will also be blessed; but those who curse them will surely be cursed."

King Balak was so angry. "I summoned you to curse my enemies, and instead you have blessed them three times! Go away. Just go home. I promised you I would reward you richly, but you have not done what I hired you to do: there shall be no reward for you. Leave my country now, while I still am willing to let you live."

Balaam shrugged. "This is what I told your messengers from the beginning: 'if King Balak were to give me his house filled with silver and gold, I still would not be able to go beyond the word of Yahweh. I would not be able to curse or bless, just by my own decision. What Yahweh tells me, that's what I will say.' That's what I told your messengers, and I said it quite clearly."

King Barak knew that this was true, but he still didn't like it. He didn't get over his anger. He didn't pay Balaam the fee. Instead, he went to his house, and worried about the coming attack. Balaam went back to his own country, to his town of Pethor on the Euphrates. But before he went, he offered one more oracle, though it was much less clear. It would be many generations before anyone would understand it. "I see someone coming, but not now or even very soon: a star arising out of Jacob, a scepter rising out of Israel." Who or what this royal person would be Balaam did not say; but he gave us the anticipation of the coming of this mighty ruler and judge.

And our people? We were unaware of all this drama until considerably later. We were not paying close attention, at the time that all this happened, for while Balaam the prophet and Balak the king were looking out at our encampments from the heights of Mount Peor, we were busy dabbling with Baal worship. It is certainly not because we deserved it, at that particular moment, that God chose to bless us instead of curse us.

Indeed, we have remained mostly unaware, through lack of paying attention, down the generations and to the present day. We scarcely knew the story of Balaam the prophet at the time, and it has remained one we scarcely know. Yet perhaps now we know it a little bit better.

11

River Jordan

> *River Jordan is deep and wide, Alleluia!*
> *Milk and honey on the other side, Alleluia!*
>
> —African-American spiritual[1]

Uncle Joshua had never heard God speak to him. Not once. Not one word. For forty years he had worked alongside Uncle Moses, watching and learning. From the time he was a young man of twenty, through his thirties and forties and fifties, he had seen Uncle Moses in action in all kinds of situations. He had heard Uncle Moses report on the things that God had said to him, and it was paragraphs and paragraphs of declarations and requirements.

But in four decades of devotion and learning, Uncle Joshua had never heard God speak to him, the way God spoke to Uncle Moses. Uncle Joshua loved God; his heart's allegiance was given to God as fully as he knew how to give it, with fervor and obedience. Yet he had not ever heard God's voice speaking to him. Not once. Not one word.

This is the story of how God began to speak to Uncle Joshua.

It doesn't always happen the same way with everyone, you know. For Uncle Moses, Uncle Jeremiah, Uncle Amos, they all heard God speak to them before they ever became leaders. Aunt Hagar heard God's voice, but never became a leader; Aunt Deborah became a leader, but no one knows any stories about when she first heard the word of God speaking to her. Yet with Uncle Joshua, he became the leader of the entire family,

---

1. William Francis Allen, Lucy McKim Garrison, and Charles Pickard Ware, eds, *Slave Songs of the United States* (New York: Simpson) 1867, #31.

and only then did he start to hear God speaking directly to him. This is the story of how that happened.

The first thing God said to Uncle Joshua was this: "Be strong, and full of courage." And not just once: God said it to him several times, like the refrain of a song. Like when the song leaders are teaching everyone a new song, around the campfire in the evening, and the song maybe has three verses and a chorus: you sing each verse just once, but you sing the chorus after each verse, and so these are the words you learn soonest and best. When that song gets stuck in your head, the words to that chorus are the words you are singing all day long. It was like God wanted those words stuck in Uncle Joshua's head: "Be strong, and full of courage."

So why do you tell someone to be brave? Because they have to do something scary. Something dangerous and frightening. Uncle Joshua was paying attention well enough to recognize that God had to be repeating this chorus over and over for a reason. There must be some anxious moments coming up.

For forty years all of our aunts and uncles had moved, as one enormous extended family, from one place to another in the wilderness. Forty years! Camp to camp, season by season, we had been a migrant people, led by Uncle Moses, and led by the glorious presence of God. Forty years of departing from Hazeroth and moving on to camp at Rithmah, then after some time departing from Rithmah and moving on to camp at Rimmon Perez, then after another period of time departing from Rimmon Perez and moving on to camp at Libnah—well, the list is much longer than that: it went on for forty years like this, camping for a while in one hard-to-pronounce place, then moving to another hard-to-pronounce place. Forty years of watching the older generation get older, and then die. Forty years of hard days of marching across the desert. Forty years of following Uncle Moses as he led us in following wherever God's presence happened to lead us next. After we had been doing this for these forty years, a whole new generation had grown up who had never known any other leader but Uncle Moses. A few of us had shadowy memories of Egypt, from our early childhood. A few more had a memory of crossing the Red Sea. But even the eldest of us had no clear memory of any leader of the family other than Uncle Moses.

For forty years, then, all of this camping and moving was aiming toward the day when we would cross the Jordan and enter into The Land. When we entered into The Land there would be no more Uncle Moses leading us. There would be no more shining glory of the pillar of cloud and pillar of fire. There would be no more wandering. We would build houses: all the aunts and uncles would have their own homes, with a roof and a fireplace and a garden. We had lived in tents as migrant shepherds for so many generations: from before we went to Egypt, and throughout much of the four centuries we were there, and now for forty more years in the wilderness. To think of becoming farmers, settled in one place: that was exciting, and scary. "Be strong, and full of courage."

Already it was happening. The good grazing land on the east side of the Jordan had caught the attention of some of the families: the descendants of Uncle Reuben and Uncle Gad and Uncle Manasseh.

By this time we mostly didn't say it that way, of course. We didn't say "the descendants of Uncle Reuben," for example. We had begun to say "the tribe of Reuben," or even just "Reuben." When we said "Reuben," we mostly no longer meant that one specific man, Uncle Reuben himself: Uncle Reuben the man was long since dead and buried, as were all his brothers, and so were all their children and grandchildren, all who had any personal memory of them; and yet the descendants of each of the twelve sons of Uncle Jacob had grown into a great extensive tribe: the twelve sons had become the twelve tribes of Israel.

These twelve tribes had arrived at a place called—

I should maybe take a moment to acknowledge that we didn't always count out the twelve in exactly the same way, because the details of how it adds up to twelve can seem a little confusing until you get used to it. The odd thing about counting the tribes of Israel has to do with Uncle Joseph and his two sons, Uncle Ephraim and Uncle Manasseh. Here is how it worked. We never really spoke of the 'tribe of Joseph' the way we would refer to the tribe of Judah or the tribe of Gad or the tribe of Simeon. Instead we would reckon it from the descendants of Uncle Joseph's two sons, Uncle Ephraim and Uncle Manasseh. They both had many descendants, enough that they could easily count as tribes themselves; but we normally referred to each of them a half tribe: the half tribe of Ephraim and the half tribe of Manasseh. Counting them that way, then, we had eleven tribes plus two half tribes: so twelve tribes in all.

But twelve refers not only to the sons and to the tribes, but also to the territories. You remember how Uncle Moses declared that the tribe of Levi would not receive a territory as their inheritance; instead, the

Lord God would be their inheritance. (What's that? Some of you don't remember? We will need to think about ways to help you remember these stories that form our heritage.) Uncle Moses had said they would have towns to live in, and the fields immediately surrounding those towns for their flocks to graze: but the tribe of Levi would never have a whole territory. Specific towns would be assigned in all the different territories. So the territory of Asher, for example, would be populated entirely by the descendants of Uncle Asher, except for several towns in that territory—Mishal, Abdon, Helkath, and Rehob, as it turns out—which were given to the Levites to dwell in as Levite towns. In the same way, several cities in each territory were set aside for Levites, with this two-part result in mind: first, so that the Levites could continue as a specified tribe of descendants of Uncle Levi down the generations, and second, so that these priestly people would always be living near at hand to all the descendants of Uncle Israel.

So there were twelve territories in all, and people have commonly reckoned this as "one territory for each tribe" or "one territory for each of the sons of Uncle Jacob." But you can see, I am sure, that it was not quite a simple one-to-one correspondence.

So. Count the sons: Reuben, Simeon, Levi, Judah, Issachar, Zebulun, Dan, Naphtali, Gad, Asher, Benjamin, and Joseph: twelve sons. Count the tribes: Reuben, Simeon, Levi, Judah, Issachar, Zebulun, Dan, Naphtali, Gad, and Asher (that makes ten), don't count Joseph yet, but do count Benjamin (that makes eleven), now add Joseph's son Manasseh (a half-tribe) and then Ephraim (a half-tribe): twelve tribes. Count the territories: Reuben, Simeon, this time don't count Levi, Judah, Issachar, Zebulun, Dan, Naphtali, Gad, Asher, Benjamin, Manasseh, and Ephraim: twelve territories. It's always twelve. If you hire a good accounting firm, they will make sure the number comes out the way you want it: "You want twelve? It's twelve."

Not long before he died, Uncle Moses gave a last big speech. Once again he told the story of how God had brought us from slavery, and provided for us in the wilderness, and established The Covenant with us. Then he began to talk about the River Jordan. "The day has come," he said, "when you will cross over the river and enter into The Land. Remember, when you get there, that it is the Lord who has given you this land. When you cross over Jordan, when you have become established in The Land, when your life is full of good things, when your flocks and

River Jordan   155

herds have multiplied in abundance, remember that it is the Lord who has given all this to you. Do not say, 'It is my own strength and my own work that has earned me all this,' for all of this is a gift that God has graciously provided. Do not say, 'It is because of my righteousness that the Lord has given me this abundance,' for you are a stiff-necked and stubborn people. It is not because of your righteousness that God gives you The Land and all its blessings: it is simply that God loves you and has chosen to bless you in this way. Do not be proud, as if your goodness has made these blessings happen. Remember what happened at Mount Sinai. There I was, up on top of the mountain, forty days of prayer and fasting in the presence of God, offering myself in full devotion while the finger of God wrote The Covenant on two slabs of stone, and at the very same time you were all down at the bottom of the mountain, casting an idol of gold and bowing down to worship it." Truly, no one has ever known how to give a scolding the way Uncle Moses could give a scolding—although my mother comes in second, and not that far behind.

One of the interesting things about Uncle Moses' speech, by the way, is this: he quoted The Covenant in it, the famous words that people sometimes call the Ten Commandments: but he didn't use exactly the same words as the ones written on the stones he had had in his hands forty years earlier, on Mount Sinai. Sometimes people suppose that it is the very words themselves that are the key, almost as if the words themselves were magic words: you have to get them exactly right or the magic won't work. But it seems your Uncle Moses didn't feel that way. Reciting these famous words that people sometimes call the Ten Commandments, he was content for the quote to be pretty close, rather than thinking he had to make it word-for-word perfect. In fact, he actually added more material to the command about observing the Sabbath day.

All right, then. The good grazing land on the east side of the Jordan had caught the attention of people from the tribes of Reuben and Gad, and the half tribe of Manasseh. The nation was going to cross the Jordan and claim all the land on the west side: but the leaders of these three portions of the family did not want to wait and see how the land might turn out to be in the territories across the river; they wanted to stake a claim to the good grazing land they could see right before their eyes.

Uncle Moses had said that that would be all right. If they wanted this land, off to the east and northeast from the rest of the family, that would be fine. Except that when it came time to fight, to possess The

Land, they still had to come along. They could not stay home in their own inheritance.

As we got ready to enter The Land, Uncle Joshua raised this same question again. We were all gathered on the east side of the Jordan. We were all standing on the land that the tribe of Reuben, the tribe of Gad, and the half-tribe of Manasseh had been granted: so they had their inheritance already. Now we had come to the decisive moment. It was time to fight for the inheritance of other people. Reuben, Gad, and Manasseh had promised they would fight on behalf of the others, back before they got their land; but now that they had gotten what they wanted, were they still willing to fight for those who had not?

It is such an important question. Will some of us be satisfied with the fact that we have obtained our share, or will we not rest until all of the family has the same satisfaction that we have? We have long struggled with this issue. What of those of us who got there first and got our portion first: what will we do? Will we ignore the needs of the rest of the family, as if the needs of distant cousins are no concern of ours? Worse than that, will we see how we can take advantage of the situation, working to make our share grow ever larger, even to the point that some of the family ends up in hunger and poverty? Or will we fight, and fight hard, to make sure that everyone will be satisfied, refusing to rest until everyone has attained to the fullness of satisfaction and Sabbath rest that our God intends for us all?

We have not always answered this question well. There have been times when the cousins descended from Uncle Judah and the cousins descended from Uncle Ephraim have fought against each other in terrible battles, where hundreds and thousands of men have been killed and their corpses have covered the battlefield. There have been times when parts of the family have forgotten that we were family at all, and have taken advantage of each other and treated each other shamefully. Although Uncle Moses insisted that we must always pay attention to those who are hungry and needy, there have been times when some cousins were starving and other cousins paid no heed, thinking it had nothing to do with them or their family.

This time, at least, the family got it right. The elders from Reuben, Gad, and Manasseh stood forth and declared that every portion of our family was solidly committed, all the way, with the whole family. Reuben, Gad, and Manasseh could not be satisfied with their inheritance until everyone else had received their inheritance, too. They were ready to fight and die to make sure that no one was left out: to make sure that all received the blessing that God intended for us.

So we came at last to the Jordan. The last time we were there, we had sent in the spies: twelve spies, one from each tribe, to scout out the land and see how to go about the conquest of the land. They came back, reporting that the land was good, but that the inhabitants looked pretty tough; it was not obvious that the conquest would be easy.

I should make it very clear that we were east of the Jordan, at this point. You can look at the map, and see that Egypt is southwest of the land of Israel; and so it's easy to assume that when we came from Egypt we would come into the land from the southwest. But that isn't quite how it happened.

We had been wandering in the wilderness for forty years, south and east of the Dead Sea: and so we came north, around the east side of the Dead Sea, and thus made our way to the Jordan River from the southeast. Just before the river we camped at a place called Sh'ttim. Perhaps the name would not matter any more than any of the long-forgotten camp sites, with names like Haradah and Makheloth and Tahath. Yet the name of this camp, Sh'ttim, would be significant, because of what happened next.

We were so close to the Jordan, at this point. Perhaps an hour's walk, no more than that. We were ready to cross into The Land, the Promised Land: the land flowing with milk and honey, the land of fulfillment. But the crossing would be difficult, because the Jordan River was at flood stage, and it was wide and roiling and dangerous.

For most of the rest of the year, the Jordan is small and tame, a shallow flow confined within narrow banks. It doesn't look like much of a river: there are lots of places where you wouldn't ford it so much as just splash your way across. When the rains come, though, it feels like all the water in the world wants to flow down that river, and what used to look like an inconsequential stream becomes a mighty flood. It is more than a mile wide, in places; and perhaps it is only thigh deep, for much of that width, yet the current is strong, and if you were to step in a hole or lose your footing, you could easily be swept away and find you were unable to get back to your feet again, you would just be tumbled and bounced in the floodwaters.

So we broke camp in Sh'ttim, and began to walk toward the river. Up ahead of us all we saw four of the priests, carrying the Ark of the Covenant. They were moving a little awkwardly, because the ground was rough and they had to carry it without actually touching it.

As you know, 'ark' is just another word for a box, a box that holds something important. The Ark of the Covenant was a large box, made of wood and covered with hammered gold. In the sunlight the gold covering seemed to glow as if it were almost alive, and it was easy to think of just how much all that gold must be worth. Yet the value of the Ark of the Covenant was not the gold that covered it, but the objects within. Inside the box were the tablets of stone on which the words of The Covenant had been etched by God: the Ten Words (sometimes called the Ten Commandments, as I've mentioned). Also inside the box were a jar of manna and the rod of Uncle Aaron. Thus this box represented our relationship with the God who had established an everlasting relationship with us, and given us food in the desert when there was no food, and protected us from our enemies.

Along the long edges of the top of the box were a series of loops. The priests threaded two long poles through those loops, one pole on each side. Thus four priests could carry the ark, one of them on each end of each pole, and none of them were directly touching it.

The first part of their job, on this day when we would cross Jordan, would be to lead the march into the river. Uncle Joshua had given them their orders: they were to carry the Ark of the Covenant out into the middle of the Jordan River, and then they were to stop there and wait, while all the nation walked past them.

Uncle Joshua had commanded it, so Uncle Joshua must have thought it would be all right. But it didn't *look* all right. It looked like they would surely get swept away. The water looked violent and angry, and how could they be expected to keep their balance against such a current? Besides, somewhere out in the middle of all that surging water was the channel, the streambed where the Jordan flowed for most of the year, and when they got to that place in the middle where they were supposed to stand and wait: why, the depth of the water would be well over their heads. Just what were they supposed to do then? I don't suppose any of them could swim; where would they have learned, in forty years of marching through the desert?

Yet "Be strong, and full of courage"—that was what Uncle Joshua had said God had told him. And Uncle Joshua had commanded them. So the four priests murmured their prayers and gathered their courage, and slowly picked their way closer and closer to the edge of that foaming muddy water.

All of our people were moving toward this spot where we would cross the Jordan, and we were all feeling worried as we saw just how dangerous fording this river would be. As we looked ahead, we saw the four priests. They were too far ahead for us to be able to hear what they might be saying to each other, but all of us could feel their anxiety. Yet that was not the most important thing that we could see. The most important thing we could see was their obedience. We could see that *that's what obedience is*. As we watched them, we understood in that moment that obedience means doing what you have been told to do, even when you are afraid.

As they walked down the last gradual slope toward the water, the miracle did not happen. At the moment when the two priests in the front were just one step away from the water's edge, the miracle still did not happen. It was not until their feet actually stepped into the water that it happened. As they carefully stepped farther and farther out into stream, the waters seemed to ease away from them, matching them step for step. The water to their left, downstream, continued to flow on down toward the Dead Sea. The water to their right, upstream, seemed to recede, leaving them picking their way across the rocks and sand. The hot desert sun began rapidly drying the surface. Soon steam was rising from the surface of scattered puddles. The four priests and the Ark of the Covenant moved steadily toward the channel in the middle of Jordan's mile-wide flow.

They got to the channel, and climbed down into the middle of the riverbed, down below our line of sight so that we couldn't see them anymore. What we could see was that the flow of the river had stopped. Just stopped. We could see the water piling up in a great heap, upstream a mile or two to our right, like a haystack or a great pile of rubble, water piled up on top of itself, waiting until the hand of God should give it permission to flow once again.

While the priests were standing there, in the middle of the Jordan watercourse, we moved on forward. We stepped out from the bank, onto the sand. Just a few minutes before, it had been tumbling waves; but now it was just damp sand, drying right up. By the time we had walked all the way across, it was powdery dry. When we got to the channel, though, we paused for a moment. Twelve elders stepped forward, one from each of the tribes. Uncle Joshua had appointed a task for them. They climbed down into the channel, and each one selected a large rock and picked it up from the river bottom. "As large a rock as you can carry," Uncle Joshua had said. So they each picked up the largest rock they could, every man struggling to get it lifted on to his shoulder, feeling the strain in his back and knowing he would be feeling the pain there for a week. They were teasing each other as they worked: "Nah, don't take that little chunk," they said to each other. "Put down that pebble and pick up a man-sized rock." And they'd point to a boulder too heavy for four men to shift, and say, "There you go. Take that one."

In the end, they had twelve large stones, well-smoothed by the river's current: hefting their stones, as they formed a line. Then Uncle Joshua led us up out of the Jordan River, and the twelve elders followed him, and all of us followed them, as we marched across the rest of the way to the other side. And there we were, in the Promised Land where we would find the rest that our God had promised us, after all those years of wandering in the wilderness.

There on the west side of the Jordan, the twelve elders set down their stones, and Uncle Joshua assembled those twelve stones into an altar. Twelve rocks, carried on the shoulders of twelve strong men: that's not enough material to build a large memorial, and yet a memorial it was. It was a memorial to help us remember: for how tragic will it be, if we forget this story? It was no great memorial tower: six stones on the bottom layer, six stones on top, and long since fallen down or worn away. It is good to establish a memorial, a reminder of important events, so that the next generation can ask, "What does it mean?" But in the end, the story and its meaning must be remembered in human hearts and told and retold with human voices.

When all of the descendants of Israel had crossed over, when all of us, from all those twelve tribes, had come to stand on firm ground in The Land, then the four priests made their way up out of the riverbed of the Jordan, and walked over to join us. Then the waters of the river began to flow once again, and behind us the Jordan was in full flood, impassible once more.

River Jordan

We marched on, just a little farther that afternoon, and camped in a place called Gilgal. Again the name of the campsite is easily forgotten, just another name of just another campsite. But again, this turned out to be a name to remember, because of what had happened just before we got there. We were now in The Land, because God had brought us there. When it seemed impossible, when the river blocking our way seemed far too deep and dangerous, our God had brought us across, and thus it was that at a place called Gilgal we spent our first night in The Land.

That Jordan River, in all its mighty power as our people saw it that day, tells us something about who we are. The stories of our family are as deep and broad as the flood of the Jordan—or deeper and broader, actually, because our stories are centuries deep and as wide as the embrace of our God. Our stories are often muddy and dangerous as well. And yet they are our stories, the stories of our family, the stories that tell us who we are as God's people.

So it would come to pass, for example, that Uncle Micah would be thinking about this story, six centuries later. So much had happened, in those six centuries: war and peace, abundance and famine, faithfulness and desolation, all of them many times over. The kingdom had been established. We had kings, kings who truly intended to serve God and then failed, with dire consequences for us all. The kingdom was split in two. Brothers and cousins hated each other, fought each other, killed each other. Time after time after time, we forgot our covenant with our God.

I have heard you, my children, in your energetic discussions of how limited human language is, for talking about God. How can any mere words capture the reality of all that is God, in a sentence on a piece of paper? So there is, I suppose, a sense in which it does not quite work to say, "We broke God's heart." Similarly with saying something like "We drove God into a towering rage, to the point of casting us off forever," or "We made God despair over whether we would ever get what the covenant was all about." Statements like these need to be taken with a little bit of judiciousness, because even though down the centuries the family has told and preserved and cherished stories that include this kind of description, we would not be wise to suppose that the way we humans feel our emotions can tell us exactly how God feels. It would be presumptuous, overstating what we know, to propose that God feels wrath or distress or heartbreak exactly like we do. Yet it has been words like these that our family has chosen, in order to describe God's feelings; and that means it would also be presumptuous for us to ignore what they said, on the assumption that somehow we know better than they did just how God felt about their situation. We are not well served, to venture into such presumption. It would be wiser for us to have the humility to reckon that our ancestors could well have had insights and experiences that we lack: and therefore to be open to the insight that God can have emotions that can be described—accurately, though not comprehensively—with terms like heartbreak or anger or despair.

So it came to pass, after the time of the judges, and after the time when the kingdom was strong, when the time came when the kingdom had been broken, indeed broken for two centuries: it came to pass that everyone's heart was turned away from God. All of us were focused only on our lives and on getting our own way. Then one day God spoke to Uncle Micah. God gave Uncle Micah a message, and so Uncle Micah went out into the middle of Jerusalem, and presented God's message in the middle of the public square.

People gathered around, as Uncle Micah began to report what God had said. He spoke in the language of the courtroom: he spoke the words that indicated that God was setting a lawsuit against us, taking us to court for breaking the covenant. How intimidating that must have been, as our people listened to God's indictment against us! "What have I done against you," God asked, "that you would treat me so badly? Come, plead your case before the mountains and the sky, and explain how this covenant got so broken. Will you say that I am the one who broke it? Search your hearts, and remember. Remember that I rescued you from being slaves in Egypt; remember than I sent Moses, Aaron, and Miriam to be your leaders on the journey. Do you remember King Balak, and what he wanted to do to you? Do you remember the words that I put in the mouth of that prophet-for-hire, Balaam? And tell me this: do you remember what took place between Sh'ttim and Gilgal? Remember these things, and you will know the saving acts that I, the Lord, have done for you."

Just a few short phrases, to recall to us these stories that we had not been remembering. But with just these brief reminders—Moses, Aaron, and Miriam; Balak and Balaam; from Sh'ttim to Gilgal—we began to remember once again. We remembered when we had fled through the desert and across the bottom of the sea, and found ourselves alive in the Sinai wilderness. We remembered the stories of Moses, Aaron, and Miriam, and how they had led us in our journey through the wilderness when God had provided water from the rock, bread from heaven, and quails—all those quails!—to keep us nourished. We remembered how our enemies intended for us to be cursed by our God and destroyed as a people, and God turned it around and blessed us instead. And we remembered what happened from Sh'ttim to Gilgal: we remembered how we had camped at Sh'ttim, after forty years of camping in one spot after another in the Sinai desert; and we remembered how we came to the River Jordan, overflowing its banks and flooding out a mile wide; and we remembered how God marched us across the riverbed on dry ground, holding back the floodwaters for us; and we remembered how God brought us on to Gilgal, where we camped on the first night that we slept in the Promised Land. We remembered the day when God brought us from Sh'ttim to Gilgal.

We remembered, and our hearts broke, and we wept.

All of the crowd was gathered around Uncle Micah, all of us filled with remorse. We remembered these stories that we had allowed ourselves to forget, and we were overcome with anguish at what our forgetting would cost us. And Uncle Micah lifted up his voice, to express that remorse for us in a great corporate lament: "What can we do, O God? What can we do, to come before you and bow ourselves down and offer a worthy sacrifice to make up for all the ways we have neglected and forgotten the covenant you have made with us? Could we offer sacrifices, bringing perfect yearling calves as a burnt offering? What can we do, O God? Could we bring thousands of prize rams? Could we offer rivers of ceremonial oil, tens of thousands of rivers? What can we do, O God? Could we—could any of us give our firstborn child for our transgression, offering the fruit of our body for the sin of our soul?"

Uncle Micah's voice had been deep and firm, so that it would carry all across the public square: full of anguish, yet strong, as he poured forth God's lament, and as he spoke for us all in our despair. But now he was silent. And all of us were silent as well, except for the sounds of quiet weeping, and quiet gasps at the dreadful thing Uncle Micah had just said.

It was true that our forgetfulness was bad. It was true that God had every right to cast us off, since we had neglected the covenant. It was true that we needed to express remorse and repentance in a serious way, if we expected to demonstrate that we truly intended to amend our ways. And yet: to offer our beloved child as a sacrifice before God? Perhaps Uncle Micah meant it as a devastatingly strong hyperbole, as it was unimaginable to put that idea into practice in real life.

In the end, though, it was God who put that idea into practice in real life. The day would come when the Messiah would stand upon the earth; and his name would be Yeshuah—Joshua, as people sometimes write it, or Jesus, as others pronounce it—and his name would mean Salvation, for he came to save us, his people, from our sins. And the day would come when he would go down to the river, and then he would come up from the middle of the Jordan to lead us all into the Land of Promise. And he, the first-born Son, would indeed be the sacrifice for the sins of our souls. But for Uncle Micah and the people of Jerusalem, those days were still to come, and indeed far in the future.

Uncle Micah rounded off this particular story by saying this: "He has told you, each of you, what is good. Now remember what it is that the Lord requires of you: to do justice, to love faithfulness, and to walk humbly with your God." His words serve as a good summary of God's call on us, as a people, as a family, as the family of God: doing justice, loving faithfulness, and walking humbly with our God.

These are not the only stories of our family. There are many more. If you look for them, you will find them.

Remember these stories, my children: listen to them and tell them, again and again. Remember the stories of our family, for these are our stories: they tell us who we are, and how we relate to one another, and how we live. Remember the stories, and the back stories; remember them in their depth and in their breadth; for they will help you remember who you are, as part of this astonishing family. Remember.